Books by Milton K. Munitz

The Moral Philosophy of Santayana (1939)

Space, Time, and Creation (1957)

The Mystery of Existence (1965)

Existence and Logic (1974)

The Ways of Philosophy (1979)

Contemporary Analytic Philosophy (1981)

Cosmic Understanding (1986)

The Question of Reality (1990)

DOES LIFE HAVE A MEANING?

Frontiers of Philosophy

Peter H. Hare, Series Editor
(State University of New York at Buffalo)

Advisory Board:

Norman E. Bowie (University of Minnesota)

Antony Flew (University of Reading, United Kingdom)

Jesse Kalin (Vassar College)

E. D. Klemke (Iowa State University)

Alice Ambrose (Smith College)

Joseph Margolis (Temple University)

Robert G. Meyers (State University of New York at Albany)

Gerald E. Myers (Graduate Center, City College of New York)

Sandra B. Rosenthal (Loyola University, New Orleans)

T. L. Short (Editor, *Academic Questions*)

Richard A. Watson (Washington University)

DOES LIFE HAVE A MEANING?

MILTON K. MUNITZ

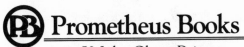 Prometheus Books

59 John Glenn Drive
Buffalo, NewYork 14228-2197

Published 1993 by Prometheus Books

Does Life Have a Meaning? Copyright © 1993 by Milton K. Munitz. All rights reserved. No part of this publication may be reproduced, stored in a retrieval system, or transmitted in any form or by any means, electronic, mechanical, photocopying, recording, or otherwise, without prior written permission of the publisher, except in the case of brief quotations embodied in critical articles and reviews. Inquiries should be addressed to Prometheus Books, 59 John Glenn Drive, Buffalo, New York 14228-2197, 716-837-2475. FAX: 716-835-6901.

97 96 95 94 93   5 4 3 2 1

Library of Congress Cataloging-in-Publication Data

Munitz, Milton K.
   Does life have a meaning? / by Milton K. Munitz.
      p.   cm. — (Frontiers of philosophy)
   Includes bibliographical references.
   ISBN 0-87975-860-0 (alk. cloth)
   1. Humanism. 2. Meaning (Philosophy). 3. Life. I. Title.
II. Series.
B821.M79   1993
144—dc20
                                         93-29529
                                           CIP

Printed in the United States of America on acid-free paper.

To Gabriel and Jesse

Contents

7

Preface

A commonly used brief formula to describe the goal of philosophy, as traditionally conceived by many, is that it seeks a critically arrived-at, unified, and comprehensive view of "the world and man's place in it." When properly fleshed out, the formula functions with reasonable success to mark the dominating interest and overall achievement of such major thinkers as Plato, Aristotle, Thomas Aquinas, René Descartes, Benedict Spinoza, Gottfried W. Leibniz, and Immanuel Kant, among others.

Two recent books of mine—*Cosmic Understanding* and *The Question of Reality*[1]—are devoted to the concept of "the world" (as this might be employed in the phrase "the world and man's place in it"), and recommend a particular way of understanding it. The present book brings to the fore and focuses on the other component in the classic formula—". . . man's place in it"—and argues for a selected way of responding to the widely posed question "Does life have a meaning?"

In carrying out the present project, I introduce and review, in appropriate detail, relevant cosmological and ontological considerations worked out in my previous books. (The argument of the present volume is self-contained and accordingly can be read independently of the others.) In this connection, I stress the importance of making a fundamental distinction between two principal dimensions of Real-

---

1. *Cosmic Understanding: Philosophy and Science of the Universe* (Princeton University Press, 1986); *The Question of Reality* (Princeton University Press, 1990).

9

ity: (1) the observable universe as the domain of interactive existents (including human existents) open to progressive inquiry, and (2) Boundless Existence, a wholly unintelligible, transcendent aspect of Reality manifested by the observable universe, though not to be confused with common theistic conceptions of God.

It is the combined presence in Reality of these two dimensions that provides the ultimate background for dealing with the foregound of human existence and for locating the possibilities for "meaning" in the lives of individual persons. The answer I propose brings together and gives appropriate, noncontradictory roles both to: (a) a type of *humanist* philosophy that assigns exclusively to human beings the choice of criteria for directing and evaluating their own lives, and (b) an intensified awareness of a level of *transcendence in Reality* that serves as the focus for a freshly recultivated sense of cosmic spirituality.

1

Does Life Have a Meaning?

THE DIVERSITY OF RESPONSES

When first encountered, certain philosophical questions have the capacity to set our minds in a whirl. What is reality? What is truth? What is the meaning of life? What is the nature of justice? of art? of mind? If one does not have a ready answer and should undertake to study the answers already given by others and to give a well-considered formulation to one's own viewpoint, it is widely attested that the prospects of *totally* eliminating the initial whirl (even for those who spend a lifetime of efforts at it) are by no means assured.

Of course there are those who, upon being confronted with one or another of the aforementioned philosophical questions, may smile at what they regard as the pretentiousness or futility of expecting there are satisfactory answers to be found at all. They will not even be provoked or enticed into a search for possible answers. There is the case, for example, of Cephalus (an elderly, wealthy, retired gentleman who makes a brief appearance at the beginning of Plato's dialogue *The Republic*) who, when asked "innocently" by Socrates, "What is justice?" declines the opportunity to engage in a dialogue aimed at finding an answer, and, as he prepares to leave, excuses himself from the surrounding company. He turns over the discussion to Polemarchus, his son and heir, and other eager young interlocutors gathered around Socrates who, unlike him, are ready to undergo what they know will be a grueling cross-examination. Cephalus takes his leave in order, as he says, "to look after the sacrifices" (to the

11

gods); it is clear he would rather spend his time *doing* what he thinks is right and just, rather than sit around and *talk* about what these concepts mean.

However, unlike countless other Cephaluses, there are those who *do* stop to try to answer the kinds of questions mentioned earlier. When provoked or stimulated by particular circumstances and experiences they have witnessed or undergone, these persons don't "leave." They stay for an answer, because to find an answer is sufficiently important, they recognize, both for themselves and for others, and takes precedence over immediate problems or what are considered matters of urgent business.

Among the questions that, once lodged in the mind of someone alive to its importance, keeps up its pressure to be taken seriously and in some way responded to, is what is commonly referred to as the question concerning "the meaning of life." One of the main reasons for its persistent or recurrent vitality is that, far from having a clear, univocal sense, it assumes protean forms, arises under different historical or personal circumstances, and voices therefore different types of need.

There are two principal ways in which questions about the meaning of life are normally couched: "Does life have a meaning?" and "What is the meaning of life?" Looked at in one way, an answer to the "what" form of the question presupposes an affirmative answer to the "does" form. Unless one agrees there is a meaning to life, it makes no sense to ask what the meaning of life is. From this point of view, an affirmative answer to the "does" form of question is logically prior to answering the "what" form, since a prior acceptance of a negative form of answer to the "does" form closes off any examination of what are the sources and types of meaning to be found. If one accepts the claims of classical pessimists, such as Arthur Schopenhauer, according to whom life is "meaningless" and must remain so (that the answer to the question "Does life have a meaning?" should be answered in the negative), then there is no point in going on to specify in what the positive meaning of life consists. The pessimist has renounced and rejected all affirmative claims that life does have a meaning. There is, of course, a possible response to the pessimist, which consists in showing that he has overlooked an important way of looking at the topic, and that his rejection of the view that life does have a meaning is premature and faulty.

Let us suppose one or another of the foregoing ways of formulating "the" question about the meaning of life were posed. Here are replies by three outstanding thinkers of the twentieth century.

Sigmund Freud wrote:

> The moment a man questions the meaning and value of life, he is sick. . . . By asking this question one is merely admitting to a store of unsatisfied libido to which something else must have happened, a kind of fermentation leading to sadness and depression.[2]

Albert Einstein wrote:

> What is the meaning of human life, or, for that matter, of the life of any creature? To know an answer to this question means to be religious. You ask: Does it make any sense, then, to pose this question? I answer: The man who regards his own life and that of his fellow creatures as meaningless is not merely unhappy but hardly fit for life.[3]

Ludwig Wittgenstein wrote:

> What do I know about God and the purpose of life? I know that this world exists. That I am placed in it like my eye in its visual field. That something about it is problematic, which we call its meaning. That this meaning does not lie in it but outside it.[4]

> The solution of the problem of life is seen in the vanishing of the problem. (Is not this the reason why those who have found

---

2. *Letters of Sigmund Freud,* trans. R. J. and T. Stern, ed. E. L. Freud (New York, 1960), 436; quoted in "Life, Meaning, and Value of" P. Edwards, ed., *Encyclopedia of Philosophy.*

3. *Mein Weltbild* (Amsterdam, Querido Verlag, 1934), translated, Sonja Bargmann, *Ideas and Opinions by Albert Einstein* (New York, Crown Publishers, 1954), p. 11.

4. *Notebooks 1914–1916,* tr. G. E. M. Anscombe (Oxford, Basil Blackwell, 1961), 72e–73e.

after a long period of doubt that the sense of life became clear
to them have then been unable to say what constituted that sense?)[5]

At first glance, the foregoing brief excerpts point to obvious
differences in viewpoint. From the hints given, are we inclined to
agree with any of the above, or should we respond quite differently?

Some philosophers question the effort devoted to finding answers
to questions about the meaning of life. They claim that the questions
as generally posed are too vague, confused, or vacuous to merit serious
attention: the "questions" are pseudoquestions. They should be
dissolved, and this would have the result that there would be no
answers to be sought, nor any to be found. Related to the immediately
foregoing deflationary position, though different in its diagnosis and
recommendation, is the view of some psychotherapists—exemplified
by Freud—who claim that while typical questions about the meaning
of life are to be dismissed as not having any genuine intellectual
interest, the act of raising such questions might nevertheless be a
symptom of a psychological disturbance, and as such should be taken
seriously: questions about the meaning of life do not call for *answers,*
they call for *therapeutic response.* The very act of raising such questions
calls for a skillful and systematic probing of its causes and a course
of treatment whose success is measured not by a clarifying and
satisfying answer given to the one raising the question, but an altered
state of psychological self-understanding and modified behavior.

MAKING SENSE OF THE QUESTION

Confronted with the foregoing variety of views and lack of consensus,
as well as the fact that statements or questions about the meaning
of life are, admittedly, very often stated in a vague and unanalyzed
way, it is obvious that the use of the phrase "the meaning of life"
requires further analysis. If questions about the meaning of life are
to be answered, we need to presuppose they are intelligible and that,
as questions, they, too, in some sense are meaningful. But what does

---

5. *Tractatus Logico-Philosophicus,* tr. D. F. Pears and B. F. McGuinness (London: Routledge & Kegan Paul, 1963), 6.521.

this amount to? It is plausible to assume that we should find, after analysis, (a) that there are several different senses of "meaning," each of which might be employed in the use of the phrase "the meaning of life"; (b) there are different types of situations that prompt the raising of questions about the meaning of life (for example, at certain major stages in the development of an individual life), or the need to confront and respond to radical upheavals in established patterns of thought and conduct at critical junctures in the shared experiences of whole groups of people. In either (or both) of the foregoing possibilities, dealing with questions about the meaning of life is tantamount to undertaking an articulation of a reflectively arrived-at philosophy of life.

A first step in examining the concept of the meaning of life consists in distinguishing several ways in which the expression "meaning" itself can be used. In everyday language, the expressions "find intelligible," "understand," and "know the meaning of" are frequently used interchangeably in a variety of situations.

In one type of situation, they are used to signify the ability *to make sense of what some linguistic or other symbol means*—of what is being communicated by its use. Thus we might be asking "What is 'life'?" One type of specialized interest in the phrase "the meaning of life" is a semantic interest in the use of the *word* "life" as it occurs in this phrase. In this case, questions about the meaning of life are to be interpreted as asking for an explanation of the use(s) of the expression "life." This type of question may arise in certain special circumstances. Thus a biologist concerned with demarcating the range of his subject matter from that of other sciences may raise this question when trying to settle the proper placement and assignment of certain borderline or controversial cases: for example, "Is a virus alive?" "Should planet Earth be classified as being a living organism (the Gaia hypothesis)?"

As distinct from the specialized interest of the biologist, there is the interest of those concerned with adopting a *philosophy of human life*. Even here it may be necessary at certain points to deal with the subsidiary question "What is the meaning of (the linguistic expression) 'human life'?" This type of question arises in considering such controversial topics as determining criteria for marking the presence or beginning of life following upon the fertilization of an ovum, or whether one should accept a belief in life after death.

While it is possible in some situations to regard the question "What is the meaning of life?" as asking "What is the meaning of 'human life'?" most people have something else in mind than the analysis of a linguistic expression. For them, to raise questions about the meaning of life is to ask for an explanation of life—of the living existence of one's own or others' life—not of a linguistic symbol. Some of the terms normally supplied to identify the kind of interest that finds expression in these questions are: "the point of it all," "significance," "value," "being worthwhile," and "purpose." Thus in asking "Does life have a meaning?" one is to be understood as asking "Does life have a value (purpose, point, significance, etc.)?" One is asking about life itself—whether *it* has a certain quality or property—not about the word "life."

In general, to ask for an explanation can point in two different directions. One direction looks backward, as it were, to the physico-chemical, biological, or other relevant *causes* that brought human life (whether that of an individual, or of the species as a whole) into existence. The other direction looks "forward": given the fact that a human life already exists, what is (are) its *value(s)*, its purpose(s), its goal(s), and how are these to be determined?

On October 17, 1989, a violent earthquake struck the area around San Francisco, California, with considerable loss of life and other major disastrous consequences. If one asks, "Why did this occur?" there is, in its fundamentals, a widely accepted scientific explanation of the causes of the event.[6] Confronted with this scientific, causal explanation, some will persist nevertheless in asking the question "Why did this occur?" since for them—mindful of the fact that many innocent

---

6. "The molten rock of the Earth's interior is covered by a rocky crust made up of plates that have been moving very slowly for millions of years, forming the continents and ocean floors. Earthquakes are most common where two plates meet. In the West, the Pacific plate has been grinding to the northwest relative to the North American plate at the rate of a half-inch a year. When stresses on a plate from deep within the Earth reach a certain point, a section lurches into a new position and the Earth quakes. The San Andreas fault along California's coast is the place where two plates meet. The fault, a complex zone of crushed and broken rock, is more than 800 miles long and extends at least 10 miles within the Earth. The segment that broke on Tuesday last ruptured in 1906 at the time of the great San Francisco earthquake." *The New York Times,* October 19, 1989, B 14.

persons perished—this catastrophe is a challenge to the faith that a moral order of Divine origin and design underlies the world's structure. In a similar circumstance, the catastrophic Lisbon earthquake of 1755 served as the occasion for Voltaire's celebrated satiric attack, in his *Candide,* on a view such as Leibniz's that "this is the best of all possible worlds." In addition to other examples, past and present, that of the Holocaust is the paradigm for those who would challenge the world picture of theism and the latter's rejection of the sufficiency of purely naturalistic, scientific (e.g., social, political, economic, cultural, historical) explanations. Consider, for example, the following testimony, which is part of the record at the Nuremberg trial, as given by S. Szmaglewska, a Polish guard at Auschwitz in the summer of 1944:

> WITNESS: . . . women carrying children were [always] sent with them to the crematorium. The children were then torn from their parents outside the crematorium and sent to the gas chambers separately. When the extermination of the Jews in the gas chambers was at its height, orders were issued that children were to be thrown straight into the crematorium furnaces, or into a pit near the crematorium without being gassed first.
>
> SMIRNOV (Russian prosecutor): How am I to understand this? Did they throw them into the fire alive, or did they kill them first?
>
> WITNESS: They threw them in alive. Their screams could be heard at the camp. It is difficult to say how many children were destroyed in this way.
>
> SMIRNOV: Why did they do this?
>
> WITNESS: It's very difficult to say. We don't know whether they wanted to economize on gas, or if it was because there was not enough room in the gas chambers.[7]

If one believes in a just and merciful God, how could this be explained? This, and many other examples pose the question already classically raised in the book of Job. It points to a human failure

---

7. Quoted, Irving Greenberg, "Auschwitz: Beginning of a New Era?" New York: KTAV Publishing House, Inc., the Cathedral Church of St. John the Divine, 1977, pp. 9–10.

to reconcile faith in God's justice, mercy, and love with what is found in experience. Unlike the reliance on scientific means or, in general, the exercise of human reason in finding adequate causal explanations for natural and human events, God's purposes are ultimately unfathomable. A belief in the existence of the latter, despite their unintelligibility to human beings, calls for faith, not for continuing inquiry and rational comprehension. The scientist is committed to the view that nature is open to progressive understanding by human means. The theist insists there are limits to human understanding that set bounds to human capacities for rendering intelligible and achieving knowledge concerning God's purposes: in their concatenation and detail, these forever and entirely lie beyond human comprehension.

In describing what it is to look for meaning of life in a broad teleological sense (as involving reference to purposes, values, goals, etc.), as distinct from explaining life in purely causal terms, I used in the foregoing a number of different terms: "purpose," "value," "significance," among others. However, it is worth noting at this point that these need not be taken as strictly equivalent. The replacement of the term "meaning" in a teleological sense by one rather than another of these supposed equivalents may yield a question that performs a different function and asks about a different aspect of life from one that makes use of a different expression on the list. For example, one may distinguish what it means to say that something has value even though there may not be some actual or discernible purpose in considering its existence or occurrence. We often attribute value to some experience that is wholly unplanned, unforeseen, and totally unexpected, the having of which was not anybody's intent or plan and thus not the outcome of anyone's purpose: such as finding a valuable object while on a leisurely stroll, even though the person was not engaged in any deliberate type of search of the sort that might characterize the governing interest of a treasure-hunter or archaeologist. Further, one may subscribe to the view that the origin of life on Earth was altogether the product of natural, "blind," causation, yet once present, could have brought with it various types of value. Consider, too, the use of the expression "the point of it all." If it is assumed that it makes sense to look for or recognize a single overarching, comprehensive "point" or purpose, it may be questioned whether there need be any such "point" as a condition for finding meaning in life. There may be a plurality of values or purposes in a person's life, without assuming they can all be unified and subsumed under some single, all-inclusive, supreme point, purpose, or value. Finally, the term "significance" in our earlier list is frequently used in such a vague and loose way, that, like the term "meaning," it can serve as a catch-all; if it is intended to clarify the term "meaning," it does not genuinely perform this function at all.

INCENTIVES FOR RAISING THE QUESTION

In examining typical occasions or conditions for raising questions about the meaning of life, there are two broad contexts to be considered. One involves the motivating sources in the life of a particular person, the other arises in the course of attempting to meet challenges and radical inroads into prevalent, inherited, fundamental beliefs, practices, and attitudes of an entire group. The group involved may range in size from a relatively small community to a very large segment of society.

There are interesting parallels between these two major contexts, but also significant differences. The occasions or conditions under which a concern with questions about the meaning of life may assume critical or urgent importance for a given individual may not be matched by a contemporaneous concern on the part of the larger community, culture, or period of history to which the individual belongs. Conversely, what may become a growing preoccupation with questions about the meaning of life for many persons need not be shared by an individual situated in their midst. Of course, there are also many situations where a preoccupation with answering questions about the meaning of life by an individual is clearly influenced by what is a prevalent interest in the same type of questions on the part of many persons. While the individual is primarily interested in finding answers that will affect the conduct of his or her personal life, the individual may look for guidance in reaching these decisions in the ways and alternatives being considered by others facing similar predicaments and in the kinds of answers they may have arrived at.

In general, whether considering an individual's life or that of a wider group (whatever the latter's size or pattern of internal identity and historical continuity), the major incentives for raising questions about the meaning of life are occasioned by major upheavals in, or changeovers from one stage or phase of life to another. The felt intensity of concern is caused by uncertainties and tensions present in leaving an established mode of life and entering upon an as-yet-untried one. The degree of concern will, of course, vary with different individuals and cultural or social groupings. In some cases, the transition may be so relatively smooth that questions about the meaning of life are either not raised at all—or minimally and with only an occasional flicker of attention—whereas in other cases the questions come to the fore with great intensity and frequency. And there are many cases that fall between these extremes. Where the changeover in goals, beliefs, and practices is so extensive and pervasive that it marks an upheaval touching virtually every aspect of life, a successful transition requires (if available) a battery of techniques and resources to restore relative equanimity and stability. If these are successfully applied toward realizing a new, meaningful pattern of life, this could be signaled by a marked reduction in, or eventual disappearance of, an explicit preoccupation with questions about the meaning of life.

Critical Junctures in the Life of an Individual

Consider the type of situation in which an individual, at a particular stage of life, is likely to raise questions about the meaning of his or her life. For present purposes, let us adopt the common division of the major stages of life into infancy, childhood, youth, mature adulthood, and old age. And let us confine attention to the last three, since these are the ones in which one normally finds, if at all, an explicit concern with answering questions about the meaning of life. (In addition, of course, to any remarks of a general character that might hold for many individuals at a particular stage of life, we should be prepared to qualify any of these in order to take into account the special circumstances—marked preoccupations, radical shifts of interests, handicaps, distinctive talents or accomplishments, and major crises—in a particular life.)

As a matter of common experience, we do well to turn to the

period of adolescence and early youth in order to find the most likely first occasions for giving serious, first-person expression to questions about the meaning of life. By then, whatever practices, beliefs, rules of action and behavior that had been transmitted, encouraged, or enforced through the agencies of the family, community, school, religious or other institutions, will have had their normal opportunities to make their strong imprint on the psyche of the growing child. For some individuals, fresh opportunities to broaden horizons in adolescence and early youth may become available through more advanced levels of education, travel, and encounters with persons belonging to different backgrounds. These experiences, along with the challenge of making career choices and selection of close associates or possible life-partners, may in turn provide the incentives for a reflective examination of what the individual hopes to accomplish in life. Further, the impact of these experiences and the need to settle on certain choices may bring with them disturbances to and conflicts with previously established patterns of behavior, accepted value schemes, and beliefs that had been instilled by parents and others. The possible clash of these inherited items with new experiences and sources of influence results in the building up of pressures that demand attention during this normally turbulent period of life.

When posed by the person at this stage of life, questions about the meaning of life are best understood as focussing on the kinds of *goals* of life that might be expected to give the person's life its meaning. The individual asks: "What, in an overall way, should be my *purposes* in the ongoing conduct of my life, and, *if* successful, what *values* do I hope to realize?" Of course, even at this stage of life the conflicts, tensions, threats, deprivations, and uncertainties already undergone by the young person—along with those suffered by members of that person's family or the wider group with which he or she associates—may be so intense and overwhelming, that the question about the meaning of life, if asked at all, is conveyed not by the "what" form, but as "Does my life have any meaning, any realistic goals that have a reasonably good chance of being fulfilled, and that could make my life worthwhile?"

For a mature adult in mid-life, the occasions and incentives to raise questions about the meaning of life generally have a different character, background of experience, and orientation from those expressed by a young person. Once again, the questions may take various forms, and are strongly influenced by the special character of the individual's past experiences. Where the character of the person's life as already lived has been shaped in part by the purposes formulated and pursued since youth, the extent to which these have yielded the hoped-for rewards and values will be judged by the individual: a balance sheet that takes note of relative successes and failures will be drawn up. Nor is this retrospective evaluation made once and for all: where repeated at different intervals, it may yield different results in ongoing life. The judgments arrived at would be based on taking note of goals hitherto pursued, opportunities seized or missed, personal health, types of encouragement and/or frustrations present in the social and physical environment, and so on. Resulting judgments could lead either to full and continued commitment to originally formulated major goals or to their modification and abandonment.

Especially in the latter cases, the conditions become ripe for once more bringing to the forefront of consciousness questions about the meaning of life. Recall Dante's opening lines of the *Divine Comedy:* "Midway in the journey of our life, I found myself in a dark wood for the straight way was lost." Entertaining thoughts about making a radical career change, major changes in lifestyle, or other types of pervasive overhauling of established patterns of personal conduct, are familiar occasions that call for the kind of soul-searching that finds its expression in a concern with questions about the meaning of life. Raising such questions is the incentive for making a renewed effort at finding answers to them. Where proposed answers are tried and found successful, the resulting changes are exhibited in the overall mode and direction of life for the individual. Classic examples of this type of situation are described in the autobiographical and biographical accounts of the lives of St. Augustine, Leo Tolstoy, John Stuart Mill, William James, and many others.

Finally, in the case of the elderly person, for whom the bulk of life has passed, the form which questions about the meaning of life assume—the relative weight given to such terms as "purpose," "value," "significance," and "worthwhileness"—shifts from what these questions were intended to convey when posed as a young person or in mid-life. Typically, a good deal of interest is directed to reminiscence, retrospection, and a gathering up, in summary evaluation, of the fruits of a lifetime of experience, expenditure of energy, and pursuit of goals. Has life been worthwhile? What have been the values realized (the accomplishments, satisfactions, creative contributions), the failures, the missed opportunities, the frustrations, the price paid for handicaps and deprivations? The emphasis shifts to actual values realized: the extent to which original or transformed goals have been satisfied and are judged to have been worth the effort in their pursuit.

In sketching the generally different circumstances that characterize the stages of life—of youth, middle age, and old age—in which one may raise the question about the meaning of life, the nature of the question itself takes on different coloring and emphasis precisely because the individual finds himself (herself) confronted with different challenges, opportunities, and the character of funded previous experience. In at least some of these types of occasions or incentives, as faced by many individuals, the person may be asking a question whose scope is of a relatively limited sort: "What do I want to do with my life, at this stage, and living in the particular social and cultural environment in which I do?" The asking of the question need not, although for some individuals it may also ask, in addition, for consideration of wider cosmic or metaphysical dimensions in which one might find some help in answering immediate personal problems.

Suffering and Death

In addition to the relatively normal occasions of a developmental sort in the life of an individual that provide the setting for raising questions about the meaning of life, there are other types of stimuli that perform the same general function.

Such, for example, is the case with the presence of suffering to an unusual and persistent degree. Although, as Buddha pointed out in his Four Noble Truths, suffering in some form is endemic to all life,[8] there are some individual lives or the shared experiences

---

8. One summary account is the following: "Birth is suffering, decline is suffering, sickness is suffering, death is suffering. To be joined with what one does not love means to suffer. To be separated from what one loves . . . , not to have what one desires, means to suffer. In short, any contact with [one of the] five *skandhas* [aggregates of the physical and psychic components of the self] implies suffering." (*Majjhima Nikaya* 1.141, quoted, Mircea Eliade, *A History of Religious Ideas*, vol. 2, p. 93.)

of an entire group in which there is a preponderance of suffering as judged by its intensity, duration, and multiple forms. It is during those periods or occasions in life when evils perpetrated by human beings on other human beings, when bodily suffering and mental anguish, when personal, social, or physical disasters have taken their toll, when death imminently threatens to terminate an incurable illness—that the cry arises in one's heart and from one's lips: "What is the meaning of life?"

Another type of incentive for raising questions about the meaning of life is the confrontation with the fact of one's own death, whether thought to be imminent or not, or in contemplating the near or remote possibility of the death of a particular social group—even that of humankind as a whole.

In the case of oneself, the need to face the inevitability of one's own death and to come to terms with it emotionally, intellectually, and spiritually, might normally arise in old age, but can also manifest itself at earlier stages of life. For example, in Plato's *Republic,* Plato puts into the mouth of Cephalus the following words, which may be taken to convey typical forebodings and uncertainties faced by many who are less than secure in their views about the "great unknown" that faces them:

> For let me tell you, Socrates, that when a man thinks himself to be near death, fears and cares enter into his mind which he never had before; the tales of a world below and the punishment which is exacted there of deeds done here were once a laughing matter to him, but now he is tormented with the thought that they may be true: either from the weakness of age, or because he is now drawing nearer to that other place, he has a clearer view of these things; suspicions and alarms crowd thickly upon him, and he begins to reflect and consider what wrongs he has done to others. And when he finds that the sum of his transgressions is great he will many a time like a child start up in his sleep for fear, and he is filled with dark forebodings.[9]

Even for an individual who believes there is no afterlife and so is not troubled by the kinds of doubts and anxieties to which

---

9. Plato, *The Republic,* translated by B. Jowett, lines 330–331.

Cephalus confesses, the question about the meaning of life may be seriously entertained, especially by a person who dwells on the fact that the light of personal consciousness will, at death, be extinguished *forever* from any possible participation in the continuation or enlarging of the range and quality of life's experiences. Focussing on this aspect of death brings with it a deepened attention to the character of conscious experience while one is still alive. One is driven to ask: "Have I given sufficient thought to judging the range and quality of life's experiences in the light of a comprehensive, critically arrived at philosophy that would guide my choices and conduct insofar as the latter lie within my power?"

Secularization and Spiritual Homelessness

From the earliest stages of human thought down to our own day (from the period in which myth was dominant to those in which cultivation and high regard for the sophisticated thought of various outstanding creative spiritual leaders and thinkers was prominent), the conviction has been widely shared that the existence of the universe calls for an explanation.[10]

According to traditional theistic religions, Divine purpose is what explains the very existence of the world; furthermore, it is the prime locus and ultimate ground for finding genuine meaning in human life. Only the genuine acknowledgment and implementation of this central belief can rescue life from futility and despair.

To the question, "Is there a ground for human existence?" as typically posed by Judaism, Christianity, and Islam, the answer is an affirmative one. There is a ground for human existence, because human beings are part of the world, and the world and all that it contains was created by God. In a theistic world picture, the phrase "ground of existence," when used specifically in connection with human existence, has reference to God's creative *causal* power and

---

10. In our own day, with the emergence of cosmological inquiry as a scientific discipline, we find a renewed concern with questions about how to explain the existence of the universe, especially as the result of what many people think is raised by the wide acceptance of the view, sponsored by many cosmologists, that the universe was (as they are prone to formulate the matter) *created* in the Big Bang.

beneficent *purpose* in giving meaning, i.e., intelligibility and value, to human life. While neither the causal power underlying the act of divine creation nor the details of divine purpose in bringing and sustaining human life in existence are known to human beings, nevertheless faith in their reality is essential to theism's belief that there is a meaning, viz., a ground for human existence.

Whereas standard answers to questions about the meaning of life had been formulated, taught, accepted, and put into practice over the course of many centuries by countless numbers of individuals adhering to one or another theistic religion in the East and West, questions about the meaning of life became a matter of deep concern (and continue to be so) for those who experience(d) what Nietzsche called "the death of God." With "the death of God," traditional versions of cosmic underpinning and divine guidance for human conduct are no longer found to be the secure haven against all doubts and uncertainties about human existence.

It is commonplace that during the last few centuries the widespread influence of science and technology has been a major factor in the growing secularization of human thought and affairs. The established patterns of thought and behavior that had permeated all aspects of life during the Middle Ages have increasingly undergone, during the entire modern period, numerous dislocations and challenges, especially through scientific discoveries in astronomy, physics, and biology. These dislocations and challenges were well under way by the sixteenth century, reached prominence in the nineteenth century, can be easily recognized in the present century, and may be expected to continue their pressure into the future until, if at all, they find their solution or abatement through the acceptance and diffusion of some widely adopted worldview and philosophy of life. In short, these developments have furnished, on a wide social and cultural level, an active seedbed for raising questions of a deeply probing spiritual character about the meaning of life.

The situation can be described, metaphorically, by saying there exists a type of hunger and homelessness that plays its own destablizing role in the lives of many individuals. This "hunger" and "homelessness" is of a spiritual sort and is, of course, to be distinguished from the material kind that is all too familiar and widespread. Unlike the latter it does not mark a social, economic, or political problem; does not arise from psychological or medical causes; is not to be solved scientifically or by the application of practical intelligence, i.e., by gathering empirical data, engaging in creative theory-construction, or formulating social policies and practical plans of action whose adequacy is judged pragmatically and by experimental tests.

In those cases where one challenges and rejects a theistic metaphysics, one thereby removes a belief in a ground for human existence as this is traditionally understood. To one who has surrendered theism as the framework for a philosophy of life, human existence will be regarded as *groundless,* and this sense of "groundlessness" may become a source of feelings of dislocation, anxiety, despair, and homelessness.

These consequences might, in turn, be removed either by finding another source for "grounding" human existence (of explaining its existence and giving a new sense of direction, purposefulness, and meaning in life) or else by dissolving and abandoning altogether the use of the very concept of finding a *ground* for human existence. In the latter case, one would not look for and hence not be disappointed in not finding a ground; there would no longer be a cause for anxiety or despair in the loss of a ground in saying that the human situation is *groundless.* Thus, if one does not relativize the use of "groundless" to the theistic notion of "ground," there would not be any incentive or need to say that life is therefore "groundless" and lacks meaning.

One possibility, of course, is to refuse to give the term "ground" a new meaning; in that case, it would make no sense to say that life either has a ground or is groundless. Still another possibility is to retain the notion of "ground" in considering the human situation, yet to give it an altogether different use from that of theistic philosophies. In that case, the question might still be raised whether, under the new definition of "ground," one should reply affirmatively or negatively to the question "Is there a ground to human existence?"

On a broad cultural front, a major incentive for giving fresh consideration to questions about the meaning of life is directly or indirectly linked to the onslaught against theism. There is, however, no uniformity in the various responses to this crisis. Instead, there are multifaceted efforts to give acceptable answers to the kinds of questions raised about "grounds" and "meaning."

The kind of need we have been describing—the sense of spiritual homelessness as the aftermath of abandoning theism, the search for newly formulated, clear, and secure grounds for finding meaning in human life—is a prevalent fact of contemporary life. It is to be found, for example, among many young adults today.

In the face of a thorough destruction of a conventional belief in God, some are driven to conclude that there is no meaning in their own or, for that matter, in other people's lives: life is absurd, in Macbeth's words, "a tale told by an idiot, full of sound and fury, signifying nothing."

On the other hand, some may enjoy a modicum of material well-being and have found their niche in the business world or in professional life. Nevertheless, such hints as they may have obtained from the scanning of philosophic literature, or the satisfactions derived from involvements in social activities and preferred channels of personal activity are insufficient to meet their innermost spiritual needs. Accordingly, many turn (or return) to the religious faith and rituals of their parents and grandparents, while others adopt a radically new pattern of religious thought and practice (for example, of an Eastern variety), while still others experiment with an eclectic synthesis culled from the foregoing.

However, for a variety of reasons, such routes to a religiously oriented spirituality are unacceptable to those who are still searching for a way to overcome their "hunger" and "homelessness." Some who recognize the prevalence of persistent feelings of despair or spiritual homelessness, reject the position of the pessimist, without at the same time recommending return to a literally interpreted, traditional faith in the existence of a divine or cosmic purpose to human life.

For some, the most attractive option for a sound philosophy of life—one to which they can give their wholehearted commitment and undertake to put into daily practice—is to be found through the adoption and pursuit of autonomously chosen purposes and standards. In a broad sense of the term, they opt for a form of humanist philosophy. The use of the term "humanism" points to a primary concern with human life, its sources, directions, and methods for achieving various types of human values through reliance on criteria devised and chosen by human beings themselves, rather than by appeal to extra-human—for example, divinely sanctioned—ones. Humanists share the propensity to look to "terrestrial" rather than otherworldly coordinates in considering the sources and goals of life. They are assured of the existence of genuine sources of meaning in life, once we redefine in what such meaning consists, and that if we put into practice the fundamental beliefs, choices, and types of attitude (the "answers") they advocate, such questions as "Does life have a meaning?" or "What is the meaning of life?" would no longer remain unsettled or continue to haunt us: doubts would be stilled, uncertainties removed.

For many, in following this orientation, the overriding and dominant purposes of a "terrestrial" and autonomously chosen sort that could provide meaning to life consist in the pursuit of selfish, hedonistic goals, in the accumulation of material goods, the exercise of power over others, or some combination of the foregoing. For others, the primary goals and values are centered in family life, whereas for others their main energies are given over to the achievement of social betterment as envisioned by some sociopolitical program or ideology. For still others, life is made worthwhile by dedication to such primary goals as the pursuit of scientific research, medical service, the creation and performance of works of art, and so on.

Uses of a World Picture

Our discussion thus far of the different forms and emphases given to questions about the meaning of life needs to be supplemented by another dimension or aspect in which they may be posed. This has to do with what may be called the relative depth or total scope with which these questions are formulated. Some probes are relatively brief, superficial, issuing in no genuine clarification, having little effect in directing or redirecting the ongoing life of the individual, or encompassing in their scope relatively little attention to anything beyond the immediate situation and problems faced in the person's own life. By contrast, others may give deeper and more sustained attention to factors and settings within which the individual's own life is situated or with which it needs to be seen as interacting: for example, of a social, historical, religious, cosmic, or metaphysical sort.

Thus, many individuals who persist in raising questions about the meaning of life, despite the relative effectiveness of any advice, reflection on personal matters, social involvements, or psychologically oriented therapeutic help, will insist that there is still something lacking in all these "answers." They may say that what they are looking for is an account of the "big picture" with whose aid they would be able to see not only their own individual personal lives, but the lives of everybody else, indeed of everything of a finite or limited sort, human or not.

Sometimes this search may be characterized as one concerned with finding a spiritual dimension to life. The expression of such a concern involves, at bottom, the appeal to a "worldview" or "world picture." This undertakes to give a description of the most inclusive setting within which human life is situated, a statement of the most fundamental beliefs and commitments on which a person may fall back in giving his account of "the world," "reality," "existence," or "being."

There is not only a wide diversity of such worldviews, but equally many differences about how one should approach the question of whether it makes any sense to look for truth or knowledge in connection with the adoption of any worldview. Some are strongly committed to the view that such metaphysical knowledge and truth can be achieved by one or another method, while others are equally convinced of the futility and vacuousness of such cognitive goals or claims. Still others take the view that rejects both the foregoing stances. For this third, "intermediate" position, having a worldview cannot yield knowledge, yet occupies an important position in humankind's intellectual economy and performs a valuable role in satisfying an ineliminable and pervasive human need.

Among those taking this last-mentioned position is Ludwig Wittgenstein. In a posthumously published book, *On Certainty* (based on notes written by him at the very end of his life), he devotes much attention to the analysis of the nature of what he calls a "world picture" (*Weltbild*)—an expression he prefers to "worldview."[11] In offering, later, my own suggestions about how to satisfy the need for a spiritual dimension in response to questions about the meaning of life, I shall outline and fall back on the support of a particular world picture (in Wittgenstein's sense of the latter expression). In order to make clear how this will be understood, let me pause briefly to review his general remarks on this topic.

According to Wittgenstein, a world picture is a set of funda-

---

11. *On Certainty*, edited by G. E. M. Anscombe and G. H. von Wright, translated by Denis Paul and G. E. M. Anscombe (Oxford: Basil Blackwell, 1969).

mental beliefs comprising a fixed framework that, for the one who adopts it, is groundless. This means that it does not rest on deeper grounds or foundations: it is not derived from and justified by appeal to other, supposedly more fundamental, beliefs or evidence. "At the foundation of well-founded belief lies belief that is not founded."[12] The metaphor of grounds or foundations is not used by Wittgenstein to recall the way in which one may use them to describe the arrangement of propositions in a deductive system for which the axioms provide the foundations of the system, and from which the remaining propositions of the system are logically derived. To capture his intention, it would be better to use the metaphor of a wall structure in a house, or a nest of twigs.

> What I hold fast to is not *one* proposition but a nest of propositions. . . . When we first begin to *believe* anything, what we believe is not a single proposition, it is a whole system of propositions. (Light dawns gradually over the whole.)
>
> It is not single axioms that strike me as obvious, it is a system in which consequences and premises give one another *mutual* support.[13]

He sometimes compares a world picture to a "scaffolding," to "an unused siding," to "a river bed."

> The propositions describing this world-picture might be part of a kind of mythology. And their role is like that of rules of a game; and the game can be learned purely practically, without learning any explicit rules. . . .
>
> The mythology may change back into a state of flux, the river bed of thoughts may shift. But I distinguish between the movement of the waters on the river bed and the shift of the bed itself; though there is not a sharp division of the one from the other.[14]

A world picture serves as the ground for other beliefs, for example, ordinary empirical judgments that are open to modification

---

12. *On Certainty,* 253. (This and other references to *On Certainty* are to numbered paragraphs.)

13. Ibid., 225, 141–142, 247–248.

14. Ibid., 91–105.

or replacement. The latter are supported by, or "rest upon" the adopted methods for justifying beliefs and fundamental commitments belonging to the world picture.

In short, in every world picture there are certain distinctions, beliefs, and principles that have the status of serving as grounds for all other beliefs, inquiries, and conceptual constructions encompassed within its scope. However, the fundamental beliefs, distinctions, and principles that serve in this capacity as grounds for other items "resting within this framework" (however tentatively), are themselves *groundless*. Being fundamental to everything else, they are not themselves derived from, or grounded in, anything more basic than themselves.

According to Wittgenstein, the only way of effecting a change in a world picture is not through attempting to *refute* a world picture different from one's own, but through what he calls "persuasion." This is not a matter of proof or evidence, since arguments, proofs, and what is acceptable as evidence rest upon, and operate within, the relatively fixed framework of a world picture. They will, therefore, be introduced or judged in different ways in accordance with the distinctive criteria and fixed commitments of different world pictures.

Differences between conflicting world pictures are not like differences and incompatibilities of a simple logical sort, such as that between "All *A*s are *B*s" and "Some *A*s are not *B*s"; nor are they like differences between empirical beliefs or judgments about "factual" matters, as in the case of conflicting reports of the results of an election for a particular candidate. They are of a different character, and concern incompatibilities in entire frameworks of beliefs. Since "reasons," "arguments," "evidence," and "proofs" may themselves be conceived in fundamentally different ways according to the groundless principles of different world pictures, it is of little avail, usually, to appeal to these in trying to adjudicate or settle differences among incompatible world pictures. If a change is to take place in the world picture already adopted, what is required is a conversion, a change in an entire outlook. Wittgenstein calls this "persuasion."

> But what men consider reasonable or unreasonable alters. At certain periods men find reasonable what at other periods they found unreasonable. And vice versa.
> But is there not objective character here?

Very intelligent and well-educated people believe in the story of creation in the Bible, while others hold it as proven false, and the grounds are well known to the former.[15]

If we accept the foregoing Wittgensteinian account of what is involved in the acceptance of a world picture, then it casts a different light on the widely accepted claim that Nietzsche's diagnosis is altogether correct that the "death of God" is at the heart of many of the upheavals of modern culture. Indeed, many would go further than Nietzsche himself by claiming that what is needed is a new, *true* metaphysics to replace the old, *false,* theistic one. From a Wittgensteinian point of view, however, the fundamental error made by those who take this latter position is that, along with adherents to traditional theistic metaphysics, they, too, look to metaphysics to give us *knowledge* or *truth* about Reality. However, no metaphysical scheme can provide such sought-for knowledge or truth. Each offers, at best, in terms of the groundless principles of a particular world picture, its own characterization of Reality and its own definitions or criteria for specifying the nature of "knowledge" and "truth." However, there is no way to "step outside" the conceptual framework of any world picture to determine what Reality is "really like" and thereby adjudicate the rival claims of different world pictures.

As Wittgenstein never tires of pointing out, however, the adoption of a world picture is not simply a theoretical matter. It is embedded in a total way of life; it informs and guides the daily activities of a person or an entire culture. This fact raises fresh questions and poses its own practical problems beyond those of a purely theoretical sort. What consequences in the conduct of our lives—its hopes, assessments, goals, efforts at controlling events, and readiness at conceding failure, or in cultivating attitudes of resignation—would accompany and follow from the adoption of a particular world picture? Are we ready to accept, in practice, the guidelines that specify "the meaning of human life" as they bear on personal and social conduct?

---

15. Ibid., 262, 608–612, 239–242, 336.

2

Scanning Existence

DIMENSIONS OF REALITY

It is commonly recognized that, once entered upon a careful analysis of a major philosophical question, it is impossible to avoid dealing with topics that at first glance would seem to lie outside the purview of the matter being addressed. This is surely true of the question concerning the meaning of life. Its hidden roots, once exposed, lead in a great number of directions: psychological, historical, religious, political, cultural, linguistic, scientific, and metaphysical, to name the most obvious.

A principal objective of the present discussion is to examine the question of the meaning of life with the aid of a number of concepts and distinctions of a broadly cosmological and ontological character.

Cosmology

The growth of scientific cosmology in our own day is a familiar story. The quantity and quality of results already achieved and the promise of more to come identify scientific cosmology as one of the most active and exciting disciplines in contemporary science. Investigations of an observational and theoretic sort, keenly followed by specialists as well as the public-at-large, mark important advances in the description and understanding of the universe. They give a clearer and more detailed picture of the structure and contents of the physical universe than had ever before been available.

To achieve, in some adequate degree, an understanding of the ever-changing, expanding frontiers of cosmological inquiry requires two-pronged attention to the work of both the cosmologically oriented observational astronomer as well as the theoretical physicist. On the observational side, this entails a study of the chief funded results and new findings concerning the major constituents of the universe—from subatomic particles to galaxies. (In connection with galaxies, it is their internal structure, processes of formation, evolutionary development, and spatial distribution that are of principal interest). On the galactic level, groundbreaking discoveries were made by Edwin Hubble in the 1920s, and these have been followed over the decades by greatly extended, detailed investigations. Similarly, in the field of subatomic (particle) physics, a vast increase in fresh observational data of crucial relevance to cosmology (the fruits of the guidance by microphysical, quantum theories and the deployment of technologically elaborate instrumentation) has been accomplished.

On the level of theory, where the principal goal is the construction of models of the universe that would both redescribe and explain empirical data already accumulated, as well as yield predictions of what might be open to further observation, the chief resource consists of *conceptual* tools. These may consist either of concepts and laws already successfully employed by mathematical physicists in other branches of physics, or of a freshly devised character in order to deal, in particular, with current cosmological problems. This side of cosmological investigation was initiated by Albert Einstein in his classic paper of 1917 devoted to the determination of the space-time properties of the universe as a whole by means of the application of the revolutionary ideas of the general theory of relativity. With this paper, Einstein launched what turned out to be a rich, rapidly expanding field of investigation that included, but also went beyond, the use of the concepts and equations of relativity physics in constructing cosmological models.

Ontology

Throughout its history, philosophy has given special attention to the use of such concepts as "existence," "the world," "reality," and "being." A standard label for this type of investigation is *ontology*. The fruits of the scientist's study of the universe are not only of great intrinsic interest, but also provide a fresh context and incentive for reexamining age-old questions dealt with in traditional theologies and philosophies. A clear challenge to work out an ontology that would help in responding to various philosophical questions brought to the fore by current investigations in cosmology provides a clear route to this domain of investigation. For one whose basic interests are philosophical in character, the study of scientific cosmology offers a challenging and promising springboard for examining traditional questions of an ontological character. By examining the philosophical aspects of scientific cosmology one hopes it would become possible to gain fresh insights, make progress in clarification of alternative views, make headway in settling some disputes, or discover new grounds for discerning genuine limits to human knowledge. In short, a revivified, intensified study by scientific means of the most comprehensive domain of all natural phenomena provides a rich fund of information and understanding that is of special interest to the philosophically minded.[16]

In the course of becoming familiar with the work of the astronomers and physicists in fashioning an acceptable conception of the universe, it would become increasingly clear (as it did for me) that in order to satisfy special philosophical interests, one cannot rest content with simply trying to master the technical vocabulary or other details of this or that model of the universe, as well as in comprehending various expository, summary accounts of established and provisional results of the work of the scientific cosmologist. One must step back from these in order to obtain the broadest perspective in the light of which one might attempt to sort out, critically examine, and decide among various options that present themselves as to how to deal with various philosophical themes.

Among the topics of a philosophical character that call for at-

---

16. My published writings on the philosophical aspects of cosmology include the following: articles on "Cosmology" in the *Encyclopedia of Philosophy* (Paul Edwards, Editor), on "Universe" in *Encyclopedia Americana* and *Harper Encyclopedia of Science;* various books, including *Space, Time, and Creation* (1957), *The Mystery of Existence* (1974), *Cosmic Understanding* (1986), *The Question of Reality* (1990); and an edited anthology, *Theories of the Universe: From Babylonian Myth to Modern Science* (1957).

tention are the possible differences from their ordinary non-cosmological meanings that affect the application of concepts such as part-and-whole, space, time, and causation when these are employed in a cosmological context. Questions about the use of such notions as "the universe as a whole," "the beginning of time," and "the creation and end of the universe" clearly beg for critical philosophical examination. If one focuses on the effort to reach an acceptable model of the universe, what can be said from a methodological or epistemological point of view about the relation of the model to the subject matter it purports to represent? If it marks an effort to discover the *truth* about that subject matter, how shall we explicate what this means? Again, what is the place of human and other forms of life in the wider scheme of things? Furthermore, is what is called "the world," "reality," or "existence," as a target for the most comprehensive investigation of an ontological sort, exhaustively defined by scientists' discoveries and conceptual constructions with respect to the physical universe? If not, what more needs to be added and clarified?

A major turning point for me in the handling of such philosophical questions as the foregoing came about as the result of making a close study of the later works of Ludwig Wittgenstein—especially the *Philosophical Investigations* (with helpful commentaries by G. P. Baker and P. M. Hacker), and *On Certainty*. I found that Wittgenstein's epoch-making contributions to the treatment of the many-sided role of language in human thought, as well as his seminal insights into the role of what he calls "world pictures," furnish the kinds of distinctions and analytic tools that can be of enormous help in constructing a world picture. As a result of the influence of the later writings of Wittgenstein, I have been drawn to a "Kantian" type of emphasis on the constructive role of language in the human mind's activities in *conferring*—insofar as it can—intelligibility on Reality.

On the ontological side, I turned increasingly to an attempt to work out a conception of Reality and a view about the nature of truth that finds more in Reality than the observable universe and its contents as depicted by cosmology. For me, at its base, the philosophy that increasingly presented its strong claims to acceptance rests on giving special recognition to *two* basic dimensions of Reality: (1) *the observable universe as a domain of interactive existents,* and (2) *Boundless Existence.*

As we shall see more fully later, the foregoing ontological distinction between two ways of treating the use of the term "existence" has a profound bearing on an attempt to respond to the question of the meaning of life.

As the setting for the life of human interactive existents, the observable universe and its variegated contents is open to increasing understanding and, in certain very special cases, to limited types of control. As parts of the observable universe, human existents have their own distinctive capacities or interactions with other existents. It is to these interactive relations that one must look for the sources, conditions, and means to *give* human life various kinds of meaning.

The capitalized expression *Boundless Existence* represents the basic ontological and epistemological fact that the very *Existence* of the observable universe (as distinguished from the type of potentially intelligible existence exhibited by any *interactive existent*) is transcendent both to any form of conceptual understanding—to the use of any scheme of *conceptual bounds*—and of course beyond even the slightest degree of human intervention or control. Boundless Existence is everywhere associated with the observable universe and its contents as an irreducible and uneliminable aspect of it, though it defeats and transcends all ordinary cognitive modes of access relying on observation or understanding.

The notion of Boundless Existence, as I employ it, is to be distinguished from the way the term "God" is employed in most theistic religions. Boundless Existence does not stand to the universe in the relation of a creative source to its created product. Nor does Boundless Existence stand to human life in the way this is construed in most theistic religions and philosophies. As viewed under the aspect of the omnipresent "emptiness" of Boundless Existence, the lives of human existents cannot find any preassigned purpose or intelligibility in the Boundless Existence of the observable universe. In contrast with theistic conceptions of God as the source for the existence of human life and the ultimate focus for a person's worship, obedience, or love (theism's standard view of the basic goals and standards for a spiritually meaningful human life), a deep awareness of the dimension of Boundless Existence enforces the conclusion that such meanings as humans can find in their lives are *not* generated by, or selectively supported and controlled by, Boundless Existence. Instead, they largely emerge from the choices and responses that human existents, as autonomous agents, make in their interactions with other *existents.*

THE OBSERVABLE UNIVERSE

A plausible route toward achieving a comprehensive perspective from which to survey the domain of interactive existents and thereby to locate human existents within its scope, is provided by the investigations of scientific cosmology.

The Observable Region and the Universe as a Whole

The observable region of the universe is the primary and immediate target of inquiry for scientific cosmology. Particularly as a result of recent achievements, there is now available a richer fund of observational data and an enlarged storehouse of conceptual tools for understanding this material than were available at all earlier periods. While the results of these scientific investigations do not suffice to yield a philosophy of human life, they provide crucially important information about, and an understanding of, the natural conditions of life that should be taken into account in any responsible articulation of a philosophy of life.

A common characterization of scientific cosmology is to say that it is a study of the universe as a whole and the large-scale properties thereof. A major problem in the clarification of the conceptual foundations of this discipline is connected with the use of the term "universe" or "universe-as-a-whole." Is the universe the same as the observed or observable universe, or should a distinction be drawn between what is open to observation and what (for various reasons) might in some sense be said to lie beyond what is observable? What are the roles played by both observation and theory in describing or construing what the universe is? Are models of the universe to be thought of as in some way articulating the structure of the universe itself? What is "the universe itself"? Is it a unique whole? Does it have a structure? Are we at all justified in making use of such a concept?

Consider, first, what to make of the use of the expression "the observable universe." Looked at in its normal employment in the context of ongoing astronomical and cosmological inquiry, what is called "the observable universe" may be regarded, for certain purposes, as an individual with a highly complex composition and structure. The description of this "individual" is a function of several factors. One of these consists in relying on the observational data gathered at a particular stage of inquiry by means of the most advanced and reliable forms of equipment. With the growth in the quantity, sophistication, refinement, and the spatial and temporal range of such probes, the addition to the store of instruments used (e.g., not only Earth-based, high-powered optical or radio telescopes, but satellite-mounted ones, supplemented by altogether new types of equipment, such as infrared and gamma-ray detectors, photo-multipliers, computer and calculating devices for refining data transmitted over vast distances from orbiting satellites, etc.), the objects, events, processes, and phenomena that are catalogued as belonging to the observable universe are not a static, once-for-all fixed assemblage. On the contrary, what the observable universe is said to be, when approached simply on an astronomical-observational level, undergoes continual modification and enlargement.

However, what is said to belong to the observable universe is not only a function of technological equipment and of the range, quality, and refinement in the observational data they provide. The descriptions and explanations assigned to the contents of the observable region, and how or where to draw the lines for the observational horizon at its outermost limits, are a function of accepted laws of nature (for example, the finite velocity of light) and of cosmological models used in interpreting observational data. In short, for cosmology, as with other empirical sciences, what is taken to be observable is never the fruit of "pure" observation. It is always encased in and accompanied by favored conceptual tools applied at a particular stage of inquiry in classifying, describing, and explaining the data. To be sure, much of this conceptual apparatus may be so firmly entrenched and traditionally sanctioned that it is virtually a fixed or minimally disturbed component in the conceptual apparatus used by all physicists. Yet even here, nothing is sacred, and revolutions in theory occur from time to time, affecting the interpretation of what is seen or measured. In any case, the kinds of changes introduced by physical theory in earlier epochs and in our own time used to interpret observational data from the observable universe, make it clear that how the latter is characterized is also very much a matter of changing *conceptual horizons* superimposed on—or, better, permeating—the specification of the ever-changing content and *observable horizons* of the observable region.

Inasmuch as the observable region, as identified for example at the present stage of inquiry, is considered incomplete when compared with some more inclusive whole that would be revealed in the course of ongoing astronomical probes, a key interest of cosmology is to anticipate, by means of the best available resources of physical theory, what the nature of this more inclusive "whole" might be. Indeed, a characteristic ambition of most theoretical cosmologists is to draw up, conceptually, a picture not simply of a *more* inclusive domain within which the known observable universe would be included as a fragmentary part, but the *most* inclusive of all physical systems to which the observable universe, as hitherto explored, belongs. In short, theoretical cosmologists are typically engaged in drawing up models of what they conceive to be *the universe as an absolute whole.*

If one were to say that in the use of the concept of the universe-as-a-whole one need not be bound by considerations of an empirical sort in choosing among different ways of specifying it, then, of course, there would no longer be any way in which one could differentiate the pursuit of cosmology as an empirical science from cosmology pursued as an exercise in mythology or pure speculation. If there is any basis for such differentiation, one must insist on the use of empirical constraints as a necessary condition in constructing and evaluating alternative, rival accounts of what is taken to be the universe as a whole.

In general, we can say that the role of observational experience in any empirically grounded science is of a twofold character. Put the matter in the context of ongoing *inquiry,* rather than in a static form of logical relations between statements. In the context of ongoing inquiry, one role of the empirical component is to initiate or prompt inquiry: to pose certain *questions,* raise certain *problems;* a second role appears toward the provisional end or relative terminus of a particular stage of inquiry: to *test predictions* of an empirical sort that have been logically or mathematically derived from the guiding principles (the distinctive, novel ideas) made use of in a given hypothesis, theory, or model. Both in its initiatory role at the outset of inquiry and at a crucial stage in providing tests that would serve to determine the correctness or incorrectness of predictions, the empirical factor plays an indispensable role in investigation. Of the two previously mentioned stages in inquiry (the initiatory and the culminating) at which the empirical factor plays a determining role, the second calls for special attention in examining the status of cosmology. For even if one can show how questions about the already confirmed observational facts about the observable universe *prompt* inquiries for an acceptable model of the universe as a whole that would, if found, answer these questions, such an achievement would be insufficient. For unless such a model leads to *testable predictions of an observational kind,* which, if confirmed, help *enlarge* the scope, details, and content of the observable universe, the claim of cosmology to be included among the empirical sciences would be seriously weakened.

Realism and Expanding Horizons

There are two broad ways in which the pursuit of cosmology—when briefly characterized as "devoted to an understanding of the universe as a whole"—can be conceived. One treats the expression "the universe" (taken as synonomous with "the universe as a whole") as a name designating the largest individual physical object or physical system that exists independently of, and antecedently to, all human observation, inquiry, conceptual interpretation, or speculation. This object or system is said to contain within its all-inclusive scope all objects and phenomena that have their own individual physical, spatial, or temporal properties. Moreover, as the most comprehensive of all physical objects and systems, the universe possesses inherently and in itself its own physical, spatial, and temporal properties—its own order. It is the goal of cosmological inquiry to disclose or discover what those properties and that order are. These properties can become known and the truth about the order set out in some form or degree. This is the view of *objectual realism.* Historically, as well as at the present time, it is the dominant view.

I shall use the expression *expanding horizons* to refer to the rival, unconventional view that would also describe in its own way the ongoing goals and actual accomplishments of cosmology. For this approach to cosmological inquiry, there need be no presupposition of the existence of an independently existing all-comprehensive object or system to be referred to as "the universe as a whole." Instead, all that cosmology as a scientific discipline can engage in is an indefinitely prolonged search for extending the limits or horizons of what is open to empirical determination. According to this approach, the goal of cosmology is to get better and better information, understanding, and knowledge of *the observable region.* Contrary to the presupposition of traditional objectual realism, it does not accept the claim there is an inescapable warrant for postulating a final, ideal terminus to the process of cognitive improvement over the indefinitely prolonged course of cosmologic inquiry. Rather, where cosmological models of the universe as a whole are entertained and evaluated, it is for their instrumental role in illuminating the observable region and making successful predictions about what would be found in the observable region. The role of cosmological models is to serve as means for enlarging our identification of the contents and scope of the observable universe, along with our understanding of how the observable region may be related to a wider whole of which it is a part.

This second mode of approach to the nature of cosmology belongs to a type of philosophy associated with the name of Immanuel Kant (1724–1804), since it was he who gave an early formulation to it in his "critical solution" to the antinomies that otherwise plague cosmological disputes.[17]

---

17. Cf. Kant, *Critique of Pure Reason,* B 546–548.

The quite general representation of the series of all past states of the world, as well as of all the things which coexist in cosmic space, is itself merely a possible empirical regress which I think to myself, though in an indeterminate manner. Only in this way can the concept of such a series of conditions for a given perception arise at all. (This cosmic series can, therefore, be neither greater nor smaller than the possible empirical regress upon which alone its concept rests. And since this regress can yield neither a determinate infinite nor a determinate finite [that is, anything absolutely limited], it is evident that the magnitude of the world can be taken neither as finite nor as infinite. The regress, through which it is represented, allows of neither alternative.) Now we have the cosmic whole only in concept, never, as a whole, in intuition. We cannot, therefore, argue from the magnitude of the cosmic whole to the magnitude of the regress, determining the latter in accordance with the former; on the contrary, only by reference to the magnitude of the empirical regress am I in a position to make for myself a concept of the magnitude of the world. . . . Since the world is not given [to] me, in its totality,

If we bear in mind that at a particular stage of scientific cosmological inquiry, the primary area of investigation is initiated by, and provisionally terminated in the identification of the observable region and the bringing to bear of the conceptual resources of a cosmological model to make that region intelligible through the use of the concept of "the universe as a whole" favored by a particular cosmological model, then we find it necessary to acknowledge the tentativeness of any account of the observable region. Not only should we recognize that at the present stage of cosmological inquiry there are differences in the community of scientific cosmologists with respect to a preferred account of the universe, but that even if some consensus should emerge that would regard, as true, some particular account, reliance on the "expanding horizons" approach would counsel that this provisionally accepted account is not likely to remain unchanged. Fresh, perhaps altogether novel, empirical and conceptual accounts of "the observable universe" are likely to emerge in ongoing inquiry.

Whatever the observational horizons or limits set by the use of available technology, and the situation of human observers at particular space-time locations, it is normally expected that with a change in such technology or space-time situation of observers, the

---

through any intuition, neither is its magnitude given to me prior to the regress. We cannot, therefore, say anything at all in regard to the magnitude of the world, not even that there is in it a regress *in infinitum*. All that we can do is to seek for the concept of its magnitude according to the rule which determines the empirical regress in it. This rule says no more than that, however far we may have attained in the series of empirical conditions, we should never assume an absolute limit, but should subordinate every appearance, as conditioned, to another as its condition, and that we must advance to this condition. This is the *regressus in indefinitum,* which, as it determines no magnitude in the object, is clearly enough distinguishable from *regressus in infinitum.*

If we wish to retain as basically sound and on the right track the main thrust of Kant's comments about the range of cosmological inquiries, we need not be confined to adopting Kant's adherence to a Newtonian philosophy of space and time, nor—given the developments since his day in astronomy, physical theory, and philosophy—need we feel obliged to describe the scope of cosmology as an empirical science in the way he recommends in his "critical solution." For example, the time-serialization he employs by which to arrange regressions or advances in examining the spatio-temporal scope of the universe, seems wholly artificial and unduly restrictive for describing the kind of progress already made or to be expected in cosmology as a scientific discipline.

range or extent of the observable region would be extended. There is no reason to believe that the presently observed region is "all there is." And where, too, the conceptual resources of a cosmological model encourage the belief that the presently observable region is part of a more extensive region whose existence and character can be inferred, and whose effects on the present observable region can be in some way observationally tested, the way is left open to consider how the already explored observable region is in *interactive causal relation* with what lies beyond its own borders. As scientific cosmological inquiry progresses on various observational and conceptual fronts, it undertakes to describe the most inclusive region open to direct, present observations, as well as the ways in which this region may be causally linked by specified, empirically confirmable, physical mechanisms with other regions in the past or that will be so linked at some time in the future. If one chooses to use the expression "universe" as a replacement for the expression "region," then one could say that one must allow the possibility that the *existent observable universe* (as identified at a given stage of inquiry) is in causal, physical interaction with other existent regions or domains.

A Conversation with Einstein

In the course of working on my book *Space, Time, and Creation* (1957), I took advantage of the opportunity to meet Einstein and to discuss with him certain themes touched on in that book. This conversation, which occurred in 1955 (three weeks before his death), was for me an unforgettable and illuminating experience.

My book dealt with a number of philosophical questions raised by the pursuit of scientific cosmology. One part of the book—a relatively small one—was devoted to a consideration of Einstein's views on the nature of space and the role of geometry in describing the universe as a whole. In that context, I not only described Einstein's distinctive philosophical views about the goals of cosmology and of science, generally, but also made some critical comments about what I took to be a certain unclarity or ambivalence in those views.

I had never met Professor Einstein before, although as with everyone else I was enormously taken with accounts of his person, achievements, and general outlook on life. Einstein certainly didn't know me, and I had no reason to believe that he would be the slightest bit interested in considering what I had to say about his philosophical views. Nevertheless, I went with my manuscript one day to the Institute for Advanced Study at Princeton. I can't be sure of the exact date, but it was at the very end of March or the beginning of April 1955. I came to the institute and told the secretary what I had in mind. And she said: "Of course I can't give you any answer. Professor Einstein gets these requests very frequently, and I can't respond positively. But if you are willing, why don't you just leave your manuscript with me. I will show it to him, and if he's interested he'll be in touch with you." I told her I was staying at the Nassau Inn for a day or two, and that I would certainly be grateful for his response. Well, soon after this, I got a phone call saying "Professor Einstein read your material and would be glad to talk with you. Where would you like to come to talk with him? Would you like to come to his house, or would you rather go to the institute?" "The institute would be fine," I replied, "if there is no objection."

I arrived at the appointed day and hour, and waited in the general lounge where people have their tea. Before long Einstein came in, and, to my surprise, went directly to me, although this was the first occasion for our meeting face to face. He asked me to accompany him to to his office. It was perhaps only for the briefest second that I had a sense that I was seeing, face to face, one of the world's greatest minds. Naturally with that sense of awe one is—at least I was—momentarily unsure how this would all go. But his manner as a person—as all those who have known him far more extensively than I ever had the privilege—will attest, he was so disarmingly gentle and accessible, that in no time whatever I felt completely at ease and remained so for the entire time (an hour or more) that I spent with him.

He began by saying that he read with interest what I had to say. I might remark that because he had this remarkable capacity at once for self-effacement, modesty, seriousness, and genuine honesty—the marks of a genuinely spiritual person—those qualities of his person communicated themselves to me in such a way that I felt that I was talking to an older, highly respected colleague.

As for the principal subject of our conversation, it revolved around a certain tension or ambivalence between a type of *epistemological realism* and a type of *conceptual constructionism* I claimed to find in his philosophical views about what science can accomplish.

Clear and enormously influential examples of realism in the history of philosophy are the philosophies of Aristotle and Spinoza. Aside from important differences between them, they are in basic agreement on one central point: when sound knowledge is achieved by human beings of some domain of natural fact, what constitutes this achievement is a *disclosure* or *discovery* of an intelligible structure embodied in an objective way in the subject matter being investigated, and present there antecedently to all inquiry. Einstein's form of adherence to realism in this broad sense was principally guided by Spinoza's espousal of this outlook.

At the same time, I detected a quite different strain, which, when put historically, stems from what we may call a "Kantian" orientation. That orientation—once again receiving a variety of special formulations—is to be found in classical statements of pragmatism, positivism, conventionalism, and some recent forms of linguistic philosophy. I felt that in Einstein's work, too, there was a strong pragmatic element displaying certain Kantian overtones, as contrasted with his dominant affinities for a realistic philosophy. The chief idea of such "Kantian-type" philosophies—I'll simply label them for present purposes as forms of *conceptual constructivism*—is that knowledge or truth, when attained, is not a form of disclosure of something already present antecedently to the exercise of human cognitive capacities, but is rather the outcome of the introduction of forms of interpretation originating in the human mind. Where successful, as judged pragmatically, the application to empirical materials of these mind-generated conceptual forms makes possible the *conferral* of intelligibility on those materials.

The combination of these two philosophies, I thought, do not sit well together and do not form in their conjunction a single consistent outlook. Einstein's response to this criticism was that he didn't think I fully appreciated his underlying motivation as a scientist. He felt that what I called his Spinozism, his realism, was a view he had to adhere to; he needed his Spinozism as his "religion."

How is this to be understood? There is, of course, one sense of "Spinozism as a religion" that was given by Spinoza himself, for example in the autobiographical remarks of his *Improvement of the Understanding*. There he argues for the thesis that one of the greatest goals and ambitions a human being can have is the exercise of his rational powers to *understand* the world in which we live. In that sense, however, there were "Spinozists" before Spinoza and since Spinoza: there are human beings for whom not the drive to power, fame, material possessions, or sensual gratifications are the central things in life, but, instead, the opportunity to understand the world. There is no question but that Einstein was a perfect example of one who adopts this "Spinozist religion."

At the same time, there is another use of the term "Spinozism." Although Spinoza (as did Einstein) rejected belief in a transcendent Creator God who is distinct from Nature, he retained a form of realism implicit in certain formulations of traditional theism. According to this realistic component of traditional theism, one aspect of God's creative handiwork consisted in the imposition of certain laws on the world at its creation. Nature accordingly possesses its own inherent, objective, necessary, determinate causal structure that awaits discovery by humans. Both Spinoza and Einstein rejected the notion of divine creation as involving the imposition of laws on Nature by a God distinct from Nature. They nevertheless retained the conviction that an understanding of Nature consists in the gradual uncovering of its own objectively existing, inherent laws. Devotion to the discovery of those laws is the supremely worthy goal of human life: to share in this devotion and practice can define one's "religion." That is Spinozism in the second sense.

It seems to me that even if one had a "Spinozist religion" in the first sense, it doesn't follow that one is obliged to adopt a "Spinozist religion" in the second sense. The second sense of "Spinozism," however, is one I also found in part in Einstein's philosophy and that I thought was not compatible with its "Kantian" strain.

Einstein claimed he needed his Spinozistic faith in the intelligibility of the world, at least psychologically, to motivate and sustain his own scientific pursuits. Unless he were convinced that there is a discoverable, rational order in the world and that it is possible to discover it (to solve the "puzzle" of existence in this way), he could not devote his entire life to scientific inquiry. While I could accept this as a *psychological* justification for his scientific pursuits, it did not seem to me to be an adequate *philosophical* justification. I argued that the two views I found in his writings did not square with one another.

INTERACTIVE EXISTENTS

That the universe exists and that we human beings, along with many other constituents, exist as parts of the universe, is accepted by virtually all world pictures, however much they may differ from one another in other respects. Nevertheless, this universal agreement can be misleading if left unanalyzed and lacking in relevant details. When supplied with such details, and particularly when seen performing its role in combination with other fundamental beliefs, major differences normally appear.

One of the ways in which the pervasive role of a philosophically articulated world picture manifests itself is in the way in which such terms as "existence," "reality," or "being" are pressed into ontological service and explicated. The concept of existence, when appearing in its nominative or closely related forms as used in everyday discourse or by philosophers, logicians, mathematicians, or scientists, has no single, standard employment. Since the term "existence" has various overlapping similarities but also differences when compared to such cognate expressions as "being," "is," "actuality," and "reality," and since, too, this concept plays a central role in our analysis, there is clear need to examine its meaning. Short of trying to survey the rich diversity of the uses of this concept, I shall, instead, simply indicate my own choices and apply them, appropriately, for the purposes at hand.

According to the world picture I am engaged in sketching, a fundamental distinction is to be made between two uses of the term "existence": (a) that which is employed in identifying and collecting examples of *interactive existents,* as normally recognized in everyday experience or in science, and (b) *Boundless Existence,* a dimension of Reality that is manifested in the observable universe and its existent contents, but whose awareness by us transcends the use of all modes of observational experience or conceptual understanding.

My principal goal is to make explicit the grounds for recognizing the foregoing distinction and to suggest its bearing on a response to the question concerning the meaning of life.

The Existence of Individuals

In approaching an analysis of the expression "interactive existent," it will be helpful to begin by considering the use of the term "exists" when it appears, grammatically, as the predicate of a sentence whose grammatical subject is an expression (e.g., a proper name) that functions as a singular referring expression for an individual object. Does the predicate term "exists" in a sentence such as "The Earth exists" ascribe the property of existence to the Earth in the same way in which, in the sentence "The Earth is spheroidal in shape," one uses the term "spheroidal in shape" to describe one of the Earth's properties?

There has been much discussion and controversy among philosophers, logicians, and others, concerning the best way to respond to this question. Some would say the subject predicate sentence in which "exists" appears as a grammatical predicate that putatively assigns the property of existence to some individual object should not be so regarded. To treat it in this way fails to distinguish it from those expressions that function as genuine predicates ascribing properties to individual entities. For the purpose of clarifying this issue, and as a basis for making an important distinction with respect to the use of the term "exists"—a distinction of which my subsequent analysis will take advantage—I propose to briefly summarize the views of the German mathematician Gottlob Frege (1848–1925), one of the principal founders of modern logic.

Frege's approach to the concept of existence follows two separate paths. In one of these (the dominant one in his writings), he denies it makes any sense at all to treat "exists" as a predicate capable of ascribing (whether truthfully or falsely) a property to an individual object, whereas on the other interpretation it makes perfectly good sense to say with respect to certain types of individual entities that they do exist. The difference stems from Frege's pursuing two different routes in the treatment of the notion of existence. When he follows the first path, he stresses what for him is an important distinction between concepts and objects. In the sentence, "Socrates is wise," the term "Socrates" designates an individual object, whereas the term "is wise," used here predicatively, marks a concept. A crucial distinction between concepts and objects is that concepts can be instantiated, whereas it makes no sense to say that an object as such can be instantiated. In the sentence "Socrates is wise," the person Socrates is an individual object to which the concept "is wise" can be meaningfully applied (whether truthfully or falsely) and therefore in which it could be found to be instantiated. Similarly, if we say "cows exist"

this is tantamount to saying that the concept "cow" has instances—
that the term "cow" can be treated predicatively—and that there are
various instances that exemplify the property of being bovine. But
since objects are not concepts, they cannot, as such, be said to be
instantiated. This approach to the notion of existence, as linked to
the notion of instantiation, is conveyed for Frege by the German
expression *es gibt* ("there is . . .").[18]

The foregoing explains the basis for the following statement by
Frege: "I do not want to say it is false to assert about an object
what is asserted here about a concept. I want to say it is impossible,
senseless to do so. The sentence 'there is Julius Caesar' is neither
true nor false but senseless."

While, for Frege, when following the instantiation (*es gibt*) route
to the treatment of the notion of existence, one cannot regard existence as as a property ascribable to an individual object, there is,
for him, another use of the notion of existence—*wirklichkeit*—that
can properly and meaningfully be predicated of an individual. Some
individuals are *wirklich: actually existent*. This is a capacity for interaction with other individual objects and for change. He writes:
"The world of actuality is a world in which this acts on that and
changes it, and again undergoes reactions itself and is changed by
them. All this is a process in time. We will hardly admit what is
timeless and unchangeable to be actual."[19] For Frege, numbers are
objective but not actual. He writes: "Of what thing are we really
asserting that it is actual if we say that there are square roots of
four? Is it 2 or –2? . . . and if I wished to say that the number 2
acts or is active or actual, this would be false and wholly different
from what I mean by the sentence, 'There are square roots of four.' "[20]

---

18. Cf. Michael Dummett, *Frege: Philosophy of Language* (London:
Duckworth, 1973), chaps. 2, 3, 4, 15; W. V. O. Quine, *Elementary Logic* (Boston:
Ginn and Co., 1941), Parts III, IV; Milton K. Munitz, *Existence and Logic* (New
York: New York University Press, 1974), chap. 4.

19. "Der Gedanke: eine logische Untersuchung," in G. Frege, *Logical Investi-
gations,* translated and edited by P. T. Geach and R. H. Stoothoff (New Haven:
Yale University Press, 1977), p. 27; cf. Michael Dummett, *The Interpretation of
Frege's Philosophy* (Cambridge, Mass.: Harvard University Press, 1981), p. 390.

20. Gottlob Frege, *The Basic Laws of Arithmetic,* translated by Montogomery
Furth (Berkeley, Calif.: University of California Press, 1967), pp. 18, 24.

Long ago, in anticipation of Frege's account of *wirklichkeit,* the foregoing description of what it means to say that something *actually exists* was given classic formulation in Plato's *Sophist.* There we find the following account given how a materialist philosopher might characterize what it means to say that something exists or has real being.

> Everything which possesses any power of any kind, either to produce a change in anything of any nature or to be affected even in the least degree by the slightest cause, though it be only on one occasion, has real existence. For I set up as a definition which defines being, that it is nothing else than power.[21]

Here we must be careful to note that whereas our normal use of the English word "power" designates a capacity to exercise force or influence over something else—to *act*—the concept "to be able," in Plato's account (from which the Greek word for "power," *dynamis,* is derived), also includes the passive capacity to receive or be susceptible to certain influences or active powers exercised by other objects. It therefore should not be restricted to the former, as is the case with a common use of the word "power" in English.[22]

My own treatment of *interactive existents* will follow Plato's characterization and, in accordance with that characterization, Frege's use of *wirklich.* It allows the ascription of a special use of the term

---

In accepting the importance of making Frege's distinction between the "there is . . ." sense of existence and the "actuality" sense, Peter Geach writes: "Actuality is attributable to individual objects; the existence expressed by 'there is a ___' is not. When we ask whether there is a so-and-so, we are asking concerning some *kind* of objects whether anything at all *is* that sort of thing; and we cannot ever sensibly affirm or deny existence, in this sense, of an individual object, any more than we can sensibly ask whether a *thing,* rather than a kind of thing, is frequent or infrequent." "What Actually Exists," in *God and Soul* (London: Routledge and Kegan Paul, 1969), p. 65.

21. Plato, *The Sophist,* 248 E, translated by H. N. Fowler (Cambridge, Mass.: Harvard University Press, Loeb Classical Library, *Plato,* vol. VII), p. 379; cf. F. M. Cornford, *Plato's Theory of Knowledge* (London: Routledge and Kegan Paul, 1935), pp. 232–239.

22. Cf. Cornford, pp. 234ff.

"exists" as a predicate to describe a property of various individual constituents of the observable universe.[23]

The term "interactive existent" may be used in a great variety of contexts. Commonly recognized, noncontroversial examples falling under the rubric of being "interactive existents" are particular physical objects and living organisms. The battery in an automobile or the person learning to read and speak Portuguese, each in its own way satisfies the requirement of being something that can act or undergo a change of state or both. The battery provides electrical power to other parts of the car (e.g., the starter mechanism, headlights, etc.); in learning Portuguese, the student acquires a certain linguistic competence and can use this acquired power, say, to read a newspaper or to order something in a restaurant. My present use of the expression "interactive existent" will be drawn, to begin with, from the domain of paradigmatic cases. In this sense, we need not hesitate to characterize individual human beings as "interactive existents."

BOUNDLESS EXISTENCE

In undertaking a philosophical inquiry about the nature and complexities of existence, any example of the account accepted of the physical universe, and therefore the one accepted at the present time (for example, the standard "Big Bang" model) is sufficient to raise such philosophical questions. This commitment allows us to ignore

---

23. It is worth remarking that the notion of "interaction" also figures prominently in contemporary quantum field theories of particle physics that are devoted to the effort to understand matter at its most elementary, fundamental level. Here, too, the entire project of describing and explaining various types of *force*—strong and weak (nuclear), electromagnetic, and gravitational—turns on discriminating the modes of *interaction* among various elementary particles (leptons, quarks, fermions, and bosons, etc.). Needless to say, it is important not to try to push this analogy too far between the notion of interactive human existents and the notion of physical forces as interactions among elementary particles. What the physicist is engaged in is the construction of a physical theory, among whose requirements is the capacity to make fruitful predictions that can be verified with a high degree of quantitative accuracy. Since my own analysis is of a philosophical character and belongs on the level of a world picture, it is not to be evaluated by the same criteria and procedures that are relevant and appropriate for a scientific theory.

(except when our interest would be of a purely historical sort) all previous cosmological accounts of the universe, whether of a scientific or a nonscientific kind. Similarly, since we have no way of anticipating what the future, indefinitely prolonged course of cosmological inquiry will produce in the way of candidates for our acceptance of how to picture the existent universe, we shall not obviously be able to use these for present philosophical purposes.

However, the fact that there is, on the expanding-horizons view of cosmological inquiry, an indefinitely large multiplicity of accounts of the universe, provides an incentive to consider broad philosophical questions about levels of existence other than that exemplified by the currently favored account of the physical universe. To put it metaphorically, the sequence of scientific conceptions of the existent universe may be looked upon as proceeding on a "horizontal" level into the indefinite future of inquiry. One conception will succeed another, perhaps absorbing certain features of the previous one in certain ways. In any case, it will both extend the fund of observational data and fashion new conceptual tools for refining and understanding the physics of the observable region.

For philosophical purposes, the thesis I shall defend is that we need not be confined exclusively to this "horizontal" level. Such confinement is appropriate for science but need not restrict the range of ontologic inquiry. In short, the proposal we shall examine is that there is also a "vertical" dimension of Reality wholly different from that which yields a scientific picture of the universe when its structure and contents are approached observationally and conceptually. What is disclosed on a "vertical" level is Boundless Existence. The awareness of this level of Reality, and a concern with bringing it into human consciousness, lies wholly beyond (transcends) the range of interests or competency of scientific cosmology.

There are several routes I shall briefly explore in amplifying the reasons for making the foregoing distinction. These have to do with: (1) clarifying the uses of the term "boundless"; (2) describing different ways in which we can be said to have what I shall refer to as a "that" experience of Existence; and (3) examining the nature of the relation between existents (whether of the universe or of human beings) and Boundless Existence.

"Boundless"

Among common uses of the term "boundless" with which I shall contrast the use of the capitalized expression "Boundless" when the latter is used in conjunction with the capitalized expression "Existence," we may distinguish, in the first place, the quantitative *geometric* sense.

Thus the term "boundless" can be used (loosely) to cover what, in a more exact way, would be meant when, in constructing a model of the universe as a whole, the cosmologist applies one or another of the three metric geometries: Euclidean, Lobachevskian, or Riemannian. In this geometric context, the term "boundless" could be understood in one or the other of two senses, (1) that which is *infinite,* and (2) that which is *unbounded.* That which is boundless in the sense of being infinite is employed in Euclidean (zero curvature, flat) geometry, or Lobachevskian (negative curvature, hyperbolic) geometry, to designate the extent of the entire space and the fact that, in such geometries, straight lines can be extended to infinity. The other sense of "boundless"—as meaning *unbounded*—is used in connection with a Riemannian (positive curvature, i.e., spherical or elliptical) geometry, which describes a space that has *no edge* and in which all straight lines (geodesics) on its surface are of finite extent. (The first cosmological model based on the theory of general relativity that Einstein proposed in 1917 made use of a Riemannian geometry: it described the universe as a whole as finite but unbounded.)

Insofar as a cosmological model typically involves the application of a specific geometric scheme, along with the use of other conceptual resources, to describe the observable region, this description cannot be said to apply to Boundless Existence: for Boundless Existence is not to be described in geometric terms at all. The Boundlessness of Existence is not to be confused with, or treated as synonymous with, a geometric property assigned to the universe in a cosmological model. Whichever of the geometric meanings of "boundless" (as infinite or as unbounded) is used in giving a geometric description of the universe as a whole according to some cosmological model, is not that intended in my use of the capitalized expression "Boundless" when conjoined with the capitalized expression "Existence." Boundless Existence eludes and transcends all conceptual descriptions, including, therefore, geometric ones.

There is another use of the expression "boundless" worth noting, which puts us on a path that could lead closer to the way I propose to use the capitalized expression "Boundless" in connection with "Existence." However, as we shall see, it, too, is not synonymous with the proposed meaning of the capitalized expression "Boundless." Thus, in connection with the expanding-horizons approach to cosmology, one may use the term "boundless," in a loose quantitative *numerical* sense, to signify an *indefinitely large number* of accounts of the observable universe and associated cosmological models that one may expect to find in the course of an indefinitely prolonged course of cosmological inquiry.

What makes this use of the term "boundless" slightly more helpful to getting at the use of the capitalized expression "Boundless" is the fact that the term "indefinitely," in the phrase "indefinitely large number" of accounts of the observable universe and associated cosmological models, points to the need to acknowledge the presence of an aspect of ineliminable ignorance, insufficiency, and indeterminateness in all human efforts to arrive at a total understanding of the world in which we live, no matter how far science may progress. There will always remain a residuum of unintelligibility about the existence of the observable universe no matter how relatively successful physical theories and cosmological models may show themselves to be. This cautionary reminder of the unavoidable limitations of human powers in understanding, suggested by the use of the phrase "*indefinitely* large" in connection with the number of conceptions of the existent universe, is of course different from the use of the term "boundless" in a purely geometric sense. Unlike the geometric meanings of "boundless," however, the term "boundless" to signify an indefinitely large number of cosmological models, does not assign a determinate property to "the" observable universe. It simply points to a persistent residuum of incompleteness and failure at understanding. And this feature of the boundlessness of cosmological inquiries, on a *horizontal* level, comes closer to, but still does not fully capture, the point of using the (capitalized) expression "Boundless."

The use of the latter expression to refer to a feature of Reality on a "vertical" level signifies the absence of *all conceptual bounds* —any and all ways of applying some set of determinate, limiting, classificatory, confining, or defining terms. On this vertical level, neither the term "boundless" in any precise (or even loose) quantitative numerical or geometric sense—nor indeed any other concept or descriptive expression—is wholly appropriate. As we shall see more fully below, the crucial aspect of Boundless Existence for human beings is the total absence of knowledge of any properties: the permanent and complete lack of all actual or possible understanding of *what* it is. With respect to Boundless Existence, there are not even degrees or elements of partial understanding of the sort to be found in accepted descriptions of the observable universe. Boundless Existence is totally impervious to all efforts at human description and understanding. In short, the use of the term "Boundless," in the phrase "Boundless Existence," needs to be distinguished not only from the geometric uses of the term "boundless," but also from the use of the same term to refer to the indefinitely large number of scientific efforts to gain an understanding of the observable universe as existent.

"That"

One special mode of access to the "vertical dimension" of Boundless Existence results from focussing on what I shall refer to as the *that* experience.[24] Here, too, as with the other distinctions previously suggested among the uses of such terms as "exist" and "boundless," I propose to use the ordinary term "that" to call attention to two different modes of human experience of the major levels of Reality.

To say that the existent observable universe exists is tautologous. However, to say that the existent observable universe Exists is not tautologous. There is a difference between, on the one hand, the use of the verb "exists" (that warrants the use of the term "existent") and, on the other hand, the use of the capitalized expression "Exists," when used as a verb, that lies behind the nominative expression "Existence" in the phrase "Boundless Existence."

The identification and knowledge of the existent observable universe involves the following factors: (a) the use of observational data; (b) the application of all sorts of conceptual schemes (mathematics,

---

24. "It is not *how* things are in the world that is mystical, but *that* it exists." Ludwig Wittgenstein, *Tractatus Logico-Philosophicus,* translated by D. F. Pears and B. F. McGuinness (London: Routledge & Kegan Paul, 1961), 6.44.

physical theory, ordinary language, world picture principles, etc.) to interpret—for purposes of description, explanation, and prediction— what is found in observation; (c) the acceptance of various propositions as true that make use of selected conceptual resources in the inter- pretation of observational data. To identify a particular scientific conception of the existent universe at a particular stage of inquiry is to involve all three factors. The use of the term "existent," in the phrase "existent observable universe," implies the acceptance of a certain account as being true and giving a successful use of specific concepts as applied to certain observational materials.

With respect to the accepted truth of the statement that the observable universe exists, one can ask such questions as: What evidence (observational, conceptual) does one have for saying that a particular account of the existent observable universe is better than some other account? If a convincing answer is forthcoming, it takes the form of upholding a new description of the existent observable universe in preference to an earlier and now-to-be-discarded one. The *that it exists* of one account of the "existent observable universe" is replaced by the *that it exists* of another account of the "existent observable universe." For example, although the standard "Big Bang" model is widely accepted at the present time, there are various features of what is regarded as "the existent observable universe" that are not adequately explained. Is there some genuinely satisfactory way of removing the singularity identified with the Big Bang? If current physics is able to give a reasonably satisfactory account of the early history of the universe up to 10^{-2} second after the Big Bang, but less secure accounts of the history of the very early universe up to the time of 10^{-43} second after the Big Bang, is there some way of giving a convincing account of what went on "before" 10^{-43} second that would make it possible to avoid using the notion of a singularity as identified with the Big Bang? How can one account for the preponderance of matter over antimatter in the universe? What is the physics underlying the formation of galaxies? How can one explain the fact that the cosmological constant has a value close to zero (that the geometry of the universe is Euclidean [flat])? What is the nature of missing (dark) matter? If any of the foregoing unsettled questions (among others) were to find widely accepted answers, they would contribute to a better account of "the existent observable universe": one would have succeeded in pushing back the present horizons of the observable universe. The preferred account of the existent observable universe would explain otherwise inadequately explained features characterizing the "*that* it exists" of the presently accepted account of the existent observable universe.

However, in connection with the awareness of Boundless Existence—that any preferred account of the existent universe is also accompanied by the awareness *that* the existent observable universe Exists—it is impossible to go beyond that distinctive experience itself. One important difference between the ontological status of any existent or collection of existents and that of Boundless Existence is that whereas existents are endlessly open to changing horizons of an observational and conceptual sort, the same cannot be said of Boundless Existence. To become aware of Boundless Existence calls for entering a different mode of experience. It is not reached by a leap of faith. Nor does it consist in a type of access that affords a special source of knowledge. It is simply a wholly unique mode of awareness that reveals a different level of Reality from that which comes from observation and the use of concepts of any sort.

The correct use of the term "Boundless Existence" lacks all reference to what is observable, conceptually interpretable, or capable of serving as subject for propositions that can be judged as true or false. It is that of which no scientifically warranted, factual knowledge at all can be obtained. Boundless Existence is unobservable, unintelligible, unknowable—beyond all space, time, or any other conceptual distinctions—hence not subject to changing horizons either of an observational or conceptual sort.

Boundless Existence is not to be confused with or identified with some preferred account of the universe as observed, rendered intelligible, or known at a given stage of inquiry. For there is no access to the "that" of Boundless Existence via the route of observation. And since an observational base is lacking, no fruitful appeal can be made to conceptual resources whose application could be empirically confirmed or rejected by reference to observational materials. If one drops all reliance on either observational data or empirically confirmable conceptual resources, then there is no way of giving a *propositional* account of the "that" of Boundless Existence. If no propositions are possible, then it makes no sense to look for truth or falsity, hence no possible *knowledge* of the "that" of Boundless Existence. In short, there is no comparable "what" or "how" to accompany the "that" of Boundless Existence that might lead to increased knowledge of Boundless Existence. All that one can have is a direct (not conceptually mediated) *awareness* of Boundless Existence. Being bereft of the appropriate use of propositional discourse that can be judged as true or false, one can only remain *silent* in one's awareness.

Neither cosmology nor any other science—nor indeed any other human resource of conceptual construction, whether myth, religion, or literature—can provide the slightest shred of genuine understanding or knowledge of Boundless Existence. No answers of the sort that one can seek or obtain in connection with the "that" experience of the existence of the existent observable universe on a scientific level of experience is forthcoming on this altogether different "vertical" level. The existence of the existent observable universe may offer various *problems* to science, many of which may, in time, be solved. The Existence of the existent observable universe is a *mystery* that neither science nor any other convincing and reliable human resource will ever succeed in removing.

Again, while what is recognized at a particular stage of inquiry as an account of the "existent observable universe" may—from the point of view of the "expanding horizons" view—be assigned to a *class* of other accounts of the "existent observable universe," Boundless Existence cannot be *classified* at all: it transcends all possible classifications. Moreover, if we say, in the special sense previously discussed, that there are many (accounts of) "existent observable universes," such multiplicity cannot be predicated of Boundless Existence. But it would also be equally misleading and inappropriate to say that Boundless Existence is *unique* in some numerical sense. Indeed, neither uniqueness nor any other predicate normally used to classify, interpret, describe, or in some other way render intelligible the subject to which it is attached can be affirmed of Boundless Existence.

From the preceding account, it should be clear that it would be wholly erroneous to assimilate the present use of the expression "Boundless Existence" to most uses of the term "God" as employed in traditional forms of theism. In the latter, the term "God" is used to refer to a personal being that transcends the world and is its Creator. It is possessed of such attributes as power; goodness;

knowledge in infinite degree; and is, for human beings, the object of total commitment, faith, worship, obedience, devotion, and love. God is supremely holy. On the present account, however, Boundless Existence is not a person, not an individual entity possessed of any attributes, whether of infinite creative power, benevolence, or wisdom. Boundless Existence is not an object of worship, obedience, or love. It is not more fundamental, ontologically, than the observable universe.

"Of"

I turn next to consider the question how we are to think of the *relation* between Boundless Existence and any example of "the existent observable universe" in an expanding-horizons view of cosmological inquiry.

Just as we are driven to recognize that no concepts can be applied in their ordinary, literal meanings to describe Boundless Existence, so, too, we must acknowledge that any attempt to describe, in a literal and wholly adequate fashion, the distinctive type of metaphysical relation that holds between Boundless Existence and the existent observable universe is also doomed to failure. For in any ordinary relation, not only can we describe or in some way identify the relata, but also the rule of use that characterizes the nature of the particular relation that holds between them can be made clear. However, since no definition or description of Boundless Existence can be given, although one may offer some account of what is taken as the existent observable universe, any purported use of a standard relation between the two must also ultimately fail. At best, only an analogical application of some standard relational expression will be possible. It is with this reservation in mind that I turn nevertheless to suggest a special type of relation that might prove helpful in approaching a discussion of the relation between Boundless Existence and the existent observable universe.

For this purpose, I choose the preposition "of." By selecting the term "of" as standing for the putative relation between Boundless Existence and the existent observable universe, we are confronted at the very outset by the following question: Is the "of" relation to be phrased as (1) "the Boundless Existence *of* the existent observable universe" or (2) "the existent observable universe *of* Boundless Existence"? Are there any significant differences between these? Is one to be preferred to the other, or may we use either, or perhaps both? Before we can undertake to respond to these alternatives, let us review the actual uses of the term "of." Here is the summary given by Webster's New International Dictionary of the English Language (second edition, unabridged).

> In the most general sense: proceeding from; belonging to; relating to; connected with; concerning. *Of* from its primary sense *from, away from* (a sense retained in its independently developed variant, *off*) had already developed in Anglo-Saxon various uses in expressions involving the idea of *moving,* or *resulting from,* as those of separation, derivation, source, agent, means, material, etc. The extension of these derived applications was much affected by its early use in translating the Latin *ab, de, ex,* and as corresponding to the French *de.* The latter influence largely brought about its use in many phrase constructions, esp. with verbs and adjectives, notably in replacing the *genitive.*

As indicated in the above, one primary, original, use of the term "of" is to suggest the idea of "resulting from," "separation, derivation, source, agent, means, material, etc." For example, it could be used "after a noun, indicating the maker or author, or when the noun is one of action, the doer, often with the force of the subjective genitive, as, the Epistles *of* Paul; the plays *of* Shakespeare; the love *of* God, that is, God's love for us" (*loc. cit.*).

If we take this group of meanings as our guide, should we think of the relation between Boundless Existence and the existent observable universe as falling within its scope, as warranting its application to the present theme? Should we say that the existent observable universe is *of* Boundless Existence, where the latter expression stands for the source or agent for the former? The analogy that springs to mind is, of course, that of God's relation to the world as described according to traditional theistic conceptions of Divine Creation in Judaism, Christianity, and Islam. The world is "of" God in the sense that the existence of, and order in, the world are derived from God. God is the Creator, Source, and Being that brought the world into existence. Should we understand the phrase "the existent observable universe *of* Boundless Existence" in a way that parallels this traditional theistic conception of Creation?

The answer is no. The relation between Boundless Existence and the existent observable universe is not one of Creation of the latter by the former. Boundless Existence is not a creator, not a person, not an infinite mind, not a being possessed of the attributes, qualities, or properties of power, wisdom, or goodness, nor indeed of any other. It does not stand to the existent observable universe and its contents in the relation of one entity (being, object, substance) to another. It is not "separated" from the world in the way in which we think of the relation between a craftsman and the work he produces.

As contrasted with the use of "of" in the phrase considered earlier to indicate a relation of *derivation* holding between the existent observable universe and Boundless Existence, should we use the expression "of," in the phrase "the Boundless Existence *of* the existent universe," in order to convey the claim that the former stands for an *attribute or property* of the latter? As Webster's points out, this meaning of "of" indicates "an attribute or distinctive mark that characterizes a person or thing—corresponding to the descriptive genitive, denoting a quality, quantity, age, price, distinguishing or specifying fact or thing, or the like, and sometimes passing into or connected with other senses; as a man *of* courage; she was all *of* a tremble; a ship *of* a hundred tons; a boy *of* ten years; etc." (*loc. cit.*). Should we regard Boundless Existence as a property of the existent observable universe? Is Boundless Existence *of* the existent observable universe?

This time our answer is not as clearly no, as was the case with the first meaning of "of." Indeed, it is an ambivalent yes *and* no. It is both since in one respect we can (with proper qualifications) affirm that Boundless Existence *is* a "property" of the existent observable universe, whereas in another respect it *is not* a property at all.

In order to explore some of the logical, ontological, and epistemic complexities whose analysis leads to a support for the foregoing claim, let me begin by recalling an earlier remark about the use of ordinary subject-predicate sentences that employ the expressions "existent observable universe," "Boundless Existence," "exists," and "Exists." I pointed out that to say "The existent observable universe exists" is tautologous, whereas the statement "The existent universe Exists" is not tautologous. The traditional, ordinary use of subject-predicate statements enshrines the distinction (recognized and systematized in Aristotelian philosophy) between individual substances (objects) and their properties. The sentence "Socrates is wise" serves as a paradigm. The subject term refers to an individual substance; the predicate term conveys a property affirmed of (applied to, as holding of) the referent of the subject term. The entire statement is true not only because the meanings of the subject and predicate terms are separately understood, but also because there is available evidence of a sufficiently strong sort to support the statement as a whole, i.e., the actual presence of the property indicated by the predicate ("wisdom") in the individual being referred to by the subject term ("Socrates").

If one employs the classical schema of a subject-predicate statement, how should we regard the use of the subject term "the existent observable universe" as a subject? Does it, too, refer to an individual object or substance? And if one uses the expressions "exist" or "Exist" in predicate position, does such use signify the assignment of a property to the subject? In the case of the sentence "The existent observable universe Exists," shall we interpret this as truly affirming a property possessed by the existent observable universe?

The use of the term "exists," in the sentence "The observable universe exists," was shown to reduce to the acceptance of certain statements in scientific cosmology as (provisionally) *true,* insofar as certain cosmological models—along with the use of various conceptual tools taken from ordinary language, physical theory, mathematics, etc.—provide a successful way of dealing with the observational data of astronomy and other empirical sources. The use of the nominative expression "the existent observable universe" merely encapsulates an accepted account, at a particular stage of inquiry, of how to describe and/or explain relevant observational materials. When "unpacked," the expression "the existent observable universe" does not designate an object or substance that has its own inherent properties apart from all human inquiry and the reliance on the complex variety of observational or conceptual resources brought to bear in such inquiry.

Similarly, I have suggested that to explicate and derive the use of the nominative expression "Boundless Existence," we had best see it in relation to the statement "The existent observable universe Exists." Consider now the subject-predicate statements "The observable universe exists" (which warrants the use of the expression "the existent observable universe") and "The existent observable universe Exists," which underlies the use of the expression "Boundless Existence." If we say "The existent observable universe Exists" or (when put in subject-predicate form, and where "Boundless Existence" functions as a *predicate*), can we say that the statement "The existent observable universe is Boundless Existence" correctly assigns a *property* to the existent observable universe? Does it make sense to think of the predicative use of the capitalized expression "Exists" (from which we derive the nominative expression "Boundless Existence") as representing a property of the existent observable universe? Should we regard the entire statement as *true?*[25]

By way of preparation for offering an answer to this question, let us first return to some relatively clear, noncontroversial cases where we are prepared to accept a statement as true insofar as by its predicate it assigns a property to the entity referred to by the subject of the statement. Once again recall our paradigm example, "Socrates is wise"—or, if there are some scruples about regarding the predicate as sufficiently well-understood—consider the statement "The Parthenon is made of marble." Both the subject term and the predicate term can be given reasonably clear, well-understood uses; the property "made of marble" is indeed a property of the subject: the entire statement is true. The proper name denotes an observationally identifiable object, a particular building; similarly, the kind of material characterized as "marble" has a commonly accepted meaning given to it by the use of an ostensive definition and other rules of use.

---

25. A similar question faces us if, instead of casting our statements in a subject-predicate form, we were to use the nominative expressions "Boundless Existence" and "the existent universe" as parts of an identity-statement. There would be no difficulty presumably—on the assumption that the terms involved are well-understood—in classifying the following as true identity-statements: "The existent universe is the existent universe," "Boundless Existence is Boundless Existence." But what about "Boundless Existence is the existent universe"? We must first overcome the objection that we should not treat the terms "Boundless Existence" or "the existent universe" as names for identifiable objects or substances and that, if regarded in this way, they cannot function as such in a true identity statement. Nevertheless, even if we were to waive this difficulty, our question would raise an equivalent problem to that faced in using the subject-predicate form, namely, whether we can say the statement "The existent universe is Boundless Existence" is a *true* statement.

If we disentangle what is involved in referring to the existent observable universe, we discover a complex, many-layered interweaving of a great variety of observationally identifiable objects, events, processes, phenomena, etc., for whose description and explanation a similarly great number and variety of conceptual resources are brought to bear. At a given stage of inquiry, not all of the statements made by a particular cosmological scheme will be accepted by those engaged in cosmological study or inquiry with the same degree of confidence and accorded the same degree of truth or certainty. Nevertheless, in this complex web of statements and cognitive claims about what is true of "the universe," there is a substantial core of reliable, commonly relied-on techniques and resources for making observational identifications of various "subjects" (e.g., galaxies, red shifts, spatio-temporal distribution and abundances of atomic species, etc.) and, similarly, a relatively stable core of conceptual resources (physical theories, classificatory devices, etc.) to warrant the truthful ascription of various properties to the fund of accumulated observational data. Although the case with affirming various properties to the existent observable universe is far more complicated and open to change, controversy, and different layers of analysis than is the case with such simple statements as the one about Socrates or the Parthenon, nevertheless one could justify and explicate what it means to ascribe certain *properties* to the subject under consideration.

What, however, about the statement "The existent observable universe Exists," or "Boundless Existence can be predicated of the existent observable universe"? Is Boundless Existence, too, a property of the existent observable universe in the same general sense in which we use the expression "property" when talking about the Parthenon and Socrates, or about the composition and structure of the observable universe—e.g., galaxies, red shifts, etc.?

The answer calls for a *philosophical* (i.e., world picture) *decision,* not for using ordinary techniques or procedures of observation or concept formation and for the application of linguistic rules of the kind found in everyday experience and in science, when these are engaged in establishing matters of fact and conveying these in true propositions. If by the term "property" is meant that which can be supported by appeals to ordinary sensory observations, measurements, etc., and the application of a verbal expression conveying a concept whose meaning rests on the appeal to ostensive definition or other types of rules, then it must be said that the expression "Boundless Existence" does *not* refer to a property in this ordinary sense. When used predicatively, the term "Boundless Existence" does not stand for a property of the existent observable universe. What it stands for cannot be found by using sensory observation, perception, or a supplementation of these provided by technologically sophisticated instruments. Nor, if one asks for a verbal definition of a concept that would set out, through the use of other, already-familiar or previously defined expressions, *what* Boundless Existence is, can one give a literal analysis of this sort. The understanding of that to which the expression "Boundless Existence" refers must be left to a type of intensified *awareness* (or, if one prefers, to "intuition," "insight," "*satori,*" "enlightenment," etc.). When one succeeds in having this awareness, it consists in disclosing what we may think of as a "property" of the existent observable universe and all that it contains. Clearly, however, such use of the term "property" is the result of making a *decision* to *extend* the ordinary use previously described. One cannot say this decision is right (or wrong), that it is true (or false). It is either accepted and employed in this extended use, or rejected. One cannot say that those who reject it are wrong or benighted. For this is only another way of saying that they do not share our world picture. In our world picture, the recognition of Boundless Existence marks a groundless ontological principle: it takes it as another basic meaning of "existence," another dimension of Reality.

Immanence and Transcendence

Having said this much, however, we must still deal with a number of further questions. One of these is the following: If Boundless Existence is *of* the existent observable universe, in the sense of being a "property" (in the extended sense) of it, does this mean that Boundless Existence can only be discussed or considered in relation to the existent observable universe? Does the identification and conceptual description of the existent observable universe have some form of *priority,* such that without the existent observable universe the use of the expression "Boundless Existence" would not have any applicability and ontologic foothold—no status at all in Reality? Is the existent observable universe a *sine qua non* for Boundless Existence? To answer this question is to invite a consideration of the bearing and relevance, if any, of the traditional terms "immanent" and "transcendent."

While Boundless Existence is an equally fundamental, irreducible *ontological* dimension of Reality, along with the use of the term "exist" to refer to what is exhibited in observational experience and the making of the latter conceptually intelligible, nevertheless the existent observable universe, for us, has a certain *epistemic* priority. Unless we *first* had the ordinary or scientific experience of the existent observable universe and its contents, we should not have the occasion or opportunity to become aware of Boundless Existence. From an epistemic point of view, as well as in considering the order in which we develop certain types of human experience, the awareness of Boundless Existence comes *later,* if at all. While ontologically of equal status with the existent observable universe, coming to recognize Boundless Existence as another and different ontological dimension involves mounting to another level of human experience; in the order of coming to know the world, it is *posterior* to observationally and conceptually encountering the existent observable universe and its manifold contents.

Is the dimension of Boundless Existence immanent or transcendent to the existent observable universe? Many traditional metaphysical or theological disputes, among naturalists, supernaturalists, pantheists, etc., that centered on whether to select one or both of these expressions in setting out their own respective worldviews, generally took their common point of departure in considering the relation of God to the world. Is God "in" the world and identical with it, or "beyond" it as its ground and source? Since most such discussions rested on a model making use of the notions of different types of "beings," "objects," "entities," or "substances," along with their putative inherent properties, this shared framework for arguing about whether God is immanent in the world or transcendent to it is not suitable and relevant for a discussion of the relation between the existent observable universe and Boundless Existence. *Neither* is to be conceived as an object or entity. Boundless Existence is not to be equated with the traditional, common conception of God as the Creator of the world. And if we adopt the expanding horizons view of cosmological inquiry (as I have proposed we do) then the existent observable universe is not to be thought of as part of a self-contained, all-comprehenisve physical object possessed of its own inherent properties. Hence there is no question to be settled whether to say one (putative) entity, Boundless Existence, is immanent in (or identical with) the other putative entity, the universe, or wholly different, apart from, and transcendent to the latter.

Once we reject and disabuse ourselves of employing the model of construing basic ontological distinctions among dimensions of existence as referring to different types of objects or entities, we may nevertheless find use for the terms "immanence" and "transcendence" in discussing the relations between Boundless Existence and the existent observable universe. Briefly, we can say *both* that Boundless Existence is in or immanent in the existent observable universe, *and* that Boundless Existence is transcendent to the existent observable universe. Bearing in mind our earlier discussion of what it means to say that we can, in an extended fashion, refer to Boundless Existence as a property of the existent observable universe, we should be justified in saying that, as such a property, it belongs to, is inherent in, is immanent in, the existent observable universe. It is not a "free-floating" property (whatever that might mean—perhaps on the analogy of Platonic Forms) that can subsist apart from the existent universe. It is inextricably bound up with and found in the existent observable universe. This much, too, was suggested by my earlier, unconventional appeal to two uses of the term "that"—one of which is involved in saying *that* the observable universe exists, and the other in saying *that* the existent observable universe Exists.

While the property of Boundless Existence is different from all other types of properties, like them it requires that we connect it with a subject (in our case, the existent universe or any of its contents) to which Boundless Existence can be assigned as truthfully describing it. Indeed, I would go further. Boundless Existence not only truthfully describes the subject, it also objectively *inheres* in the subject; belongs to it, whether or not we recognize Boundless Existence as doing so. Whereas all other properties, as observationally identified or described through the use of humanly conditioned perceptual apparatus or humanly constructed linguistic (conceptual) devices and rules, are dependent on and throughout linked to the human factor in distinguishing properties and formulating true statements, the same is not the case with the property of Boundless Existence. It does not depend on the operation of human equipment or cognitive apparatus of any sort. It is *there.* It is an uneliminable, objective, ontological property of the existent observable universe, however the latter is construed. It is a basic dimension of Reality.

On the other hand, there is also good warrant for saying that Boundless Existence is transcendent to the existent observable universe. For if, as we have argued, the identification and description of the existent universe involves the use of human observational and conceptual resources, the same cannot be said of our coming to be aware of Boundless Existence. That which this term points to cannot be observationally identified, conceptually described, or explained in any way. It transcends all such normal human powers and accomplishments. It is wholly other, "beyond" the existent observable universe.

Summary

In summary: If we use the terminology of "that" and "what" (what in traditional metaphysics was referred to as the distinction between existence and essence), then we can say that in the case of Boundless Existence its "what" coincides with, and is identical with, its "that." There is no description, definition, or conceptual analysis possible of Boundless Existence, since to give these is to make use of various ways of stating "what"; but there is no "what" to Boundless Existence. Its "what" is not distinct from its "that," and its "that" is indescribable, unanalyzable conceptually, and indefinable. Yet "Boundless Existence" is another way of saying "The observable universe Exists." To say this is to assign this unique property or "what" to the observable universe. It has the property of Existence. But this property is not further analyzable, describable, explainable, or definable. In this respect, Existence is different from existence. The observable universe exists: it is an existent. So is every object, event, and phenomenon in the observable universe. In the case of existents, one can probe into what its existence amounts to. For an existent, there is a difference between its "what" and its "that" (or, in older terminology, a distinction between its essence and its existence). Substitute for "essence" not the term "universal," but the term "general predicative expression, part of a constructed human language, used to describe, explain, and analyze the properties of objects and events encountered in experience," and one can make a distinction between the meaning and applicability of such general predicative expressions and the individuals to which they are applied in discourse. No such distinction is possible for Boundless Existence, or—what amounts to the same thing—the way in which the term "Exists" is used as a predicate or concept to describe the property of the observable universe.

With respect to an ordinary existent, the predicates used to describe or explain it can either be retained as true of the individual to which it is applied, or withdrawn in favor of some other, preferred conceptual account. However, no such options are available in using the expression "Exists" as a predicate. In this sense, Boundless Existence is not replaceable except by discarding the world picture with which it is associated. If one does retain the world picture in which it plays this groundless role, then, in that world picture, it is not further analyzable or open to an improved and more detailed account.

3

The Locus of Meanings

INTERACTIVE MEANINGS

We have cast our net widely, and now we have come home. From our brief cosmic explorations and ontological probes, have we brought back any insights that might be of help in answering the question with which we started, viz., "Does life have a meaning?"? Do our previous surveys and analyses help bring into sharper focus an attitude toward life that is more satisfactory than the one with which we may have set out? Has our journey yielded results that can fill the special type of void and meet the spiritual need experienced by many persons?

On its ontological side, the conception of Reality (world picture) I have sketched has, as a main feature, the drawing of a distinction between two levels of existence: (1) the existent observable universe as the domain of interactive existents, and (2) Boundless Existence. In the previous chapter, we explored some of the ways in which we might undertake to describe the relation between these two dimensions. As a possible tool for this project, we brought into play some of the common uses of the expression "of." By taking into account the distinctive ontological status and character of each dimension, and by bearing in mind the several uses of "of," we were able to suggest some of the different ways in which we may think of the relation between the existent observable universe as the domain of interactive existents and Boundless Existence. In particular, we considered whether (or in what sense) the domain of interactive

73

existents is "of" Boundless Existence, or Boundless Existence is "of" the observable universe as the domain of interactive existents.

In the light of this analysis, what can we say, in particular, about ourselves as *human existents?* Let me put the question preanalytically by using the common preposition "in." If we were to use the phrase "man *in* existence," as marking a relation of some sort, how could this relation be specified? How would a continued reliance on the fundamental ontological distinction between (1) the observable universe as the domain of interactive existents and (2) Boundless Existence, affect the use of "in" in the phrase "man in existence"? Would this provide any valuable clues toward articulating a philosophy of life? For example, should we expect to find meaning in our existence only insofar as we are located "in" the broad domain of the observable universe of interactive existents and as characterized by our own distinctive spatial, temporal, physical, chemical, biological, psychological, and culturally influenced properties? Or, if we maintain that (along with the observable universe and all its contents) we, too, participate "in" the ontological dimension of Boundless Existence, how would this affect our search for meaning?

The key concept of *actuality* (the exercise of power) that Plato's materialist recognized, and that Frege also identified as one of the meanings of "existence" (the other being what he called the *es gibt* sense), plays an important role in the response to the question of the meaning of life I shall be offering in what follows. The notion of "interactive human existents" (that builds on the Plato-Frege conception of "actuality") offers a key route for analyzing our main theme. It invites attention to factors frequently overlooked or insufficiently stressed in some standard and popular accounts.

One of the immediate benefits of taking as our point of departure the underlying schema for the manifold ways in which human existents interact with other existents (whether human or nonhuman) is that, in *filling out the schema* in various ways, we are discouraged at the very outset from looking for an answer that would be couched in terms of high levels of generality. By paying special attention to the details of how the schema is filled out, we should be discouraged from looking for a general statement purporting to describe what (or whether) there is "a" meaning, "the" meaning, the "ultimate" meaning, or perhaps "none at all," in what is commonly referred to, in a global way, as "human life." Discussions, controversies, and summary judgments about the meaning of life, when couched in such general terms, very often turn out to be vacuous and unilluminating. They start at a high level of abstraction and generality and very often remain on the same level of abstraction and generality, leaving it except perhaps for some examples here and there. Rarely do they earn their keep from having emerged from lower-level, detailed examinations of specific instances that fall within the scope of a great number of "parameters" and "coordinates," whose specification and exemplification would be necessary in a fruitful analysis. Instead of talking in the most general terms about whether "life" is or is not "ultimately meaningful (or meaningless)," a more fruitful approach is not shackled at the outset by relying on broad generalities in the search for an answer. In being everywhere encouraged to see how to fill out the schema of "interactive human existents," one looks instead for plural *meanings* in *individual lives* and in the manifold ways in which a person interacts with other existents.

I shall later contrast the outcome of this type of approach with what can be said when the question about "the meaning of life" is considered under the aspect of Boundless Existence. Since Boundless Existence is not an existent, we shall find that the "location" of human existents "in" Boundless Existence is essentially different from that which holds for any interactive relation between human existents and other existents "in" the existent observable universe. I shall accordingly reserve for later examination the question of how to describe the relation between human existents and Boundless Existence in its bearing on the question of the meaning of life.

A Simple Schema

Let us adopt the following simple formula as a convenient way of stating the general schema to be investigated:

$$e_h \longleftrightarrow e$$

The symbol "e_h" represents one or more human existents; the symbol "e" represents one or more existents, whether human or not; the symbol $\longleftrightarrow$ represents the interaction between the human existents and other existents involved in any given instance of an interaction; it is the locus or source of meanings for the human existents engaged in the interaction.

Since this last-mentioned factor (the interaction of human existents with other existents, including other human existents) is the locus and source of *meanings,* it is of central importance in the present analysis. Let me pause, therefore, to clarify in a preliminary way how I shall use this expression in distinction from, but also in relation to, other common uses of the expression "meaning."

One whole class of uses of the term "meaning" has to do with its role in the study of the functioning of human languages. Roughly, it concerns the conventionally accepted uses of an expression (word, phrase, sentence, etc.) as these are adopted and applied by those who have some competence in a particular natural or technical language. In an extension of this primarily linguistic use of the term, the word "meaning" can also be used in connection with the intentions conveyed, or the understanding achieved, with respect to types of humanly constructed symbolic representations other than those that are purely linguistic (e.g., the iconography of a painting, ceremonial gestures, etc.).

Nevertheless, despite its centrality and importance in the analysis of language and other types of symbolic representation, this meaning of the term "meaning" will not be of primary concern in the present examination of the question of the "meaning" of life. Here we are concerned with human actions and interactions of varied types, rather than with linguistic or symbolic meanings, and the way in which the manifold variety of such interactions between human existents and other existents can be the basis for special types of meaning associated with them. While some of these interactions may be of a linguistic sort, most of those we shall be concerned with extend far beyond that limited subclass.

Another common use of the term "meaning" is to signify someone's *purpose* or *intention.* When used in its nominative form ("the meaning of . . . is"), it is closely related to the use of the verb "to mean (such-and such)," i.e., as signifying an intention to communicate something by means of language or to achieve some end through some action. Leaving aside the purely linguistic context in which this may be employed, the use of "to mean" or "meaning," as signifying an intention to achieve a certain purpose in engaging in some action or behavior, comes closer to the use of "meaning" I wish to isolate, yet is still not fully equivalent to the latter. For, when put in temporal terms, the use of "meaning," in the sense of "intending," has a future-looking orientation—to something which may or may not be accomplished—whereas, if put in temporal terms, the sense of "meaning" I wish to emphasize is associated with the *actual* occurrence, whether in the past, present, or over a stretch of time, of an (actual) interaction between a human existent and other existents.

Again, the sense in which I shall use the expression "meaning(s)," has to do with that which is located in the consciously appreciated or recognized interaction between a human existent and other existents, and, as such, is to be distinguished in certain respects from what is also frequently referred to as a matter of "meaning" for someone's life. Thus, one might say that the fact that individual *A* happened to be at a particular place at a certain time, or was in contact with another person, etc., played an important role—had important *consequences*—in *A*'s life: it had great "meaning." However, this use of the term "meaning" may be used in such a way that *A* may not have been conscious of the importance of that encounter or interaction either at the time it occurred or at any later time in that person's life. Perhaps the "meaning" (the "importance") was recognized by others—e.g., a psychotherapist, biographer, or someone else, using their own preferred methods for understanding the "causal structure" of events. Indeed, it might be claimed that a certain interaction, encounter, or experience was undergone, guided, or absorbed into a person's life history in an "unconscious" way, or on a "subconscious" level, by the individual. From the point of view of the present analysis, however, this latter use of "meaning" (as allowing for an importance in judging a person's life, even though it is never brought before the attention of the person in question) is different from the one I am engaged in explicating. For, according to the latter, in order to be meaningful or have meaning for a human existent, it is necessary for the individual human existent participating in a particular interaction with other existents, to be consciously aware of that meaning at some time in his or her life. Of course, a person may not appreciate that "meaning" at the very moment the interaction with some other existent is taking place. It may come later (under prodding by, or as benefitting from, the insights of someone else) or, perhaps even by the person himself or herself as a result of later reflection and understanding. And if the particular interaction or experience does become conscious for the individual in this or some similar way, then I should want to say it serves to mark an interaction that *does* carry *meaning* for the given individual.

We come, finally, to another common use of the term "meaning" that comes closer to any of the foregoing discriminated senses of this term in suggesting the sense in which a "meaning" is determined by an actual interaction of a human existent with other existents. This common use has the sense of the *import* of such-and-such, or what is also sometimes suggested by the use of the term *significance*. To raise the question about the import or significance of someone's experience as actually undergone is to raise a question about its *"import"-ance,* again, rather loosely and vaguely, about its *value*. In what follows, it is these latter directions that I wish to pursue in investigating the way in which interactions of human existents and other existents serve as the bearers of meanings in the life of individual persons.

Filling in the Schema

A human existent is a distinctive, complex structure of various inter-connected mechanisms for interacting with other existents in the world in which it lives and has its being. As interactive existents, humans are enormously more complicated than any other known interactive existents. This is not to deny, of course, that nonhuman existents have their own depths of complexity. Atomic nuclei, various types of molecular compounds, stars, galaxies, eukaryote cells, plants, animal species, higher primates, etc., provide typical subject matters endlessly investigated by specialized scientific disciplines. The fruits of these inquiries contribute in their own way toward understanding relevant aspects of the structure and functioning of humans, since a human existent possesses physical, chemical, or biological properties which it shares in certain respects with objects on each of these other levels. For example, as an animal, a human being has the capacities to feed and reproduce, to use organs of sense perception, to feel pain, and to participate in the activities of a social group.

Nevertheless, human beings also have distinctive powers that not only obviously differentiate them from nonhuman existents, but also from higher primates and early hominids. They develop complicated types of language to serve various needs, adopt (as well as undergo change in) beliefs; guide behavior and practical action in accordance with beliefs; form specialized social groupings, produce works of art; create advanced forms of technology; engage in scientific inquiry; and satisfy capacities for wonder, feeling, imagination, and spirituality in various ways. If we follow Plato's account of existence as the possession of powers to act or be acted on (*dynamis*), then it is clear that human existents share many powers with other nonhuman existents; within the class of human existents, some powers (the so-called generic ones) are shared by virtually all human existents, while other powers are possessed by a relatively small group, and still others are "unique."

In order to fill out in an elementary inductive fashion the plurality of types of meanings in the lives of individual human existents that can be accommodated within the simple schema for interactive human existents, let us consider some typical parameters and coordinates. Let me venture on a short list of my own for such parameters and coordinates. Though it possesses no great systematic power or impressive credentials, to be sure, perhaps it has enough to suggest where one might look to see the complexity and variety of particular examples that each item on the list might yield.

There is, first of all, the whole domain of purely bodily interactions, grounded in the physical, physiological, structures with which (or specially dependent on which) an interaction, for a particular human existent, is mediated with other object(s) or person(s). These include the sense organs, nervous system, musculature, specialized digestive and sexual organs, among others. Hammering a nail, following the track of a moving animal or automobile, uttering a warning shout, reciting a poem, conducting an orchestra, and countless other acts of varying degrees of simplicity or complexity, clearly engage and depend on one or a combination of our bodily organs and structures. Thus, a person handicapped and suffering from some deficiency is unable (temporarily or permanently) to interact with, and therefore to be open to, certain kinds of meanings that are possible for others.

Another large, rich category collects examples belonging to the domain of arts and crafts, where one may participate as creator, performer, observer, or student. Closely related is the great variety of esthetic responses made by an individual and perhaps communicated to others.

Science and technology is another area of dominant and growing importance in the modern world, in which the lives and channelled experience of many individuals find a special niche and role.

Think, too, of such varied social structures as family, community, nation, clubs, gangs, professional organizations, businesses, sports, games, hospitals, educational and religious institutions, and so on, which provide the setting for daily, regular, or intermittent and occasional involvements and interactions.

Each area or a combination of these, as particularized over the course of an individual life, is where one finds innumerable examples of interactions whose kind, number, quality, and degree of importance provide *meanings* to an individual's life.

The modes of interaction, the mechanisms involved, the levels on which these operate and perform, the extent to which those exemplified in the life span of a particular individual are also found in other human lives—all of these are open to wide variation. The factors that determine the degree of commonness or relative uniqueness are many: genetic, environmental, cultural, and so on. Moreover, among these interactions, some are accompanied by consciousness on the part of the individual, while others are not so accompanied at any point in the life of that individual.

In examining the great variety of interactive linkages between a human existent and other existents as the locus for meanings, one way of describing such linkages is in terms of whether they are primarily *cognitive* or engage the *feelings* (affects).

With respect to the cognitive side of human capacities, a basic distinction is that between capacities that engage various organs and mechanisms of *perception,* and those that bring into operation the powers for *conceptual understanding.* Specialized organs and mechanisms for seeing, hearing, etc., belong to the former group, whereas special human powers for the formation and articulation of concepts (as conveyed in language and applied in a great variety of circumstances), belong to the latter group. There are, of course, many lines of interconnection between these two groups to be found in the circumstances and activities of everday life, as well as on the more specialized and sophisticated levels of art, science, technology, and the management of public affairs. Further, there are many forms of interaction between perception and conception as each of them makes its own distinctive contribution to *imagination* in the latter's various forms—for example, in dreams, personal memories, and the exercise of creative imagination in science, literature, and the arts.

Examples from the domains of perception, conceptual understanding, or the interplay of the inputs of these in imagination, are multitudinous: they can be simple, familiar, or of varying degrees of complexity, arcaneness, and novelty. At one end of the spectrum are such everyday, widely shared examples as hearing a thunderclap, experiencing the sweet taste of sugar, petting a dog or cat, while on more sophisticated and less widely shared levels of perception, there is the experience of attending an elaborately staged performance of a major opera, or being called upon as a professional wine taster to make comparative evaluations of different vintages, or undertaking, as an expert on the works of a particular classical painter, to determine the authenticity of a particular work of art. Similarly, on the level of conceptual understanding and the use of language, again the range of examples covers a wide spectrum. At one end, there are such commonplace instances as a young child's understanding of the meaning of "spoon," how to add a column of figures, or an adult's understanding of travel directions, and at the other end, such highly specialized achievements as mastering the complicated proof of Gödel's theorem,[26] tracking the details of the human nervous system, or understanding Kant's *Critique of Pure Reason*. In the case of imagination, once again there are countless examples of relatively commonplace experiences of image production such as one finds in engaging in private, brief reminiscences, or in the construction of a simple bed-time story to entertain a child. At the other extreme, are such products of creative imagination as Einstein's creation of the theory of relativity, Joyce's composition of *Ulysses,* and Bach's writing of the *St. Matthew Passion.*

---

26. According to which no significant formal system can ever be strong enough to prove or refute every statement it can formulate.

In the case of interactions by a human existent with particular objects or persons that produce primarily affective meanings, as distinguished from primarily cognitive ones, an emotional response, in some degree of intensity on the part of the interactive human existent, is present as its most notable feature.

For many influential thinkers in the history of philosophy, the role of feeling in human experience is regarded as potentially harmful unless subordinated, controlled, or in some situations altogether replaced by the products of reason. The affects are "inadequate ideas" or "confused perceptions" that need to be replaced, wherever possible, by the more "adequate ideas" and guiding principles of reason.

For example, Descartes wrote:

> Love, hate, fear, anger, etc. . . . . as merely affections or passions of the mind . . . are confused thoughts which the mind does not have from itself alone, but because it is intimately united to the body, receiving its impressions therefrom. For there is the greatest difference between these passions and the distinct thoughts which we have of what ought to be loved, chosen, or shunned [although they are often found together].[27]

And Leibniz wrote:

> Sensuous pleasures are really confusedly known intellectual pleasures. Music charms us, although its beauty only consists in the harmonies of numbers and the reckoning of the beats or vibrations of sounding bodies, which meet at certain intervals, reckonings of which we are not conscious and which the soul nevertheless does make. The pleasures which sight finds in proportions are of the same nature; and those caused by the other senses amount to almost the same thing, although we may not be able to explain it so distinctly.[28]

In contrast with the foregoing, my own approach would recognize emotively charged interactions as sources for meanings in life, without assigning them a subordinate or inferior role in the range of meanings

---

27. *The Principles of Philosophy,* Part IV, Principle CXC.
28. *The Principles of Nature and of Grace, Based on Reason,* sec. 17.

and without requiring that they be subjected in every case to the control and approval of reason. Here are typical examples of affective meanings: a parent's delight at watching a very young child taking its first steps; the deep sadness and concern felt in witnessing widespread cases of disease-ridden and starving children or homeless individuals in various parts of the world; exhiliration at solving a difficult and challenging puzzle or problem; undergoing shock upon discovering the loss of a much-treasured object; as a performer, being stirred by the appreciative applause of an audience; the grief felt on the death of a close relative or friend; and so on.

According to the present analysis, an interaction that does not involve consciousness for the individual engaged in an interaction has no meaning for that individual: to recognize "meanings" as arising from interactions between existents requires consciousness. Although in our formula the arrow marking the interaction between existents points in both directions, it is only from the side of those existents that manifest or possess consciousness that meanings can be appreciated or identified. While, in principle, even higher levels of animal existents other than humans can appreciate meanings, they do not have the conceptual powers to discriminate them as such. Hence, as far as we know, it is only human existents who have the requisite degree or type of consciousness, including especially conceptual and linguistic sophistication by which to talk about, evaluate, classify, and appreciate meanings. We shall therefore confine ourselves to the way in which interactions among existents will have, at least at the crucial pole of such interactions, *human* existents. Of course, where the other pole of the interaction also represents one or more human existents, the appreciation of meanings, marked by the interaction between human existents who are situated "at both ends of the arrow," will work from either or both directions.

Consider the following: the participation and ongoing reactions by members of a string quartet in performing a piece of music, a family's picnic, the responses by residents of a community undergoing a tornado's attack and its devastating aftermath, an audience listening to a lecture by a highly respected authority.

In any particular situation of interaction, shall we think of the symbol for "human existent" as representing one individual person, or can it also be used in the plural as standing for a group (whether small or large) of human existents? Another way of phrasing our question is to ask whether the consciousness of meaning in a particular instance of human interaction with other existents is, at bottom, located in a single person's experience, or can it also be distributed among several different individuals and shared by them, in various ways, in the same situation? It is true, of course, that where there are several (or even a large number of) individuals sharing in, or undergoing, a certain event, the degree of sharing or similarity of response may range from near "identity" or uniformity (for example, of great joy or horror, or of illuminating clarity, depth, etc.) to more varied and lesser amounts or shades of agreement, including perhaps some wholly dissenting voices about the "real meaning" of the event. Yet even here, the several judgments of meaning as held by different participants in a given event are not a fixed and irrevocable matter; these are subject to change with ongoing experience, retrospective coloring and reevaluation in the light of more mature insight and the benefits of an extended perspective that time itself makes possible for the individuals involved. As the qualitative markers for particular, temporally located interactions by human existents with other existents, "meanings" can themselves undergo change in the consciousness of an individual over the course of time in the life of that individual.

This brings me to a point worth stressing in more general form. Whatever the degree of sharing among individual human existents, each of whom finds some "meaning" in a given interactive experience, it turns out that, at a more fundamental level than the communal one, the finding and judgment of meaning with respect to some particular interaction is a matter for each individual, as conscious, to specify and decide. The finding of meanings in life is an exercise that only a particular person can perform and judge, whatever the input or sharing in such meanings by others. It is the individual person's own conciousness whose life is under self-scrutiny that is a fundamental ingredient in determining the meaningful interactions of that individual in the course of his or her life.

If it is necessary that an individual human existent for whom some interaction has some meaning be conscious of that meaning, are we to say that all meanings are therefore *subjective?* To introduce the latter expression recalls long and interminable debates among philosophers—when discussing esthetic, moral, or other types of value—

about whether one should say that such meanings are "subjective" or "objective." I do not wish to rehearse here the many bypaths, variations, and viewpoints of those participating in such debates. It should be obvious from our own approach thus far to the analysis of meanings that we need not get embroiled in debates of these types. The very framework and requirements of our approach to meanings does not encourage the debate to get started by polarizing the discussion between those who uphold subjectivism and those who defend objectivism.

Insofar as we take seriously—as I surely propose we do—the notion of *interaction* between a conscious human existent and other existents as the locus and source of meanings, the option of choosing between subjectivism and objectivism in characterizing the meaning found or undergone *does not even arise*. If by "subjectivism" is meant that whatever value, importance, or (as I prefer to label it) "meaning" is present, this presence is to be assigned exclusively to what the human subject brings to, creates, and judges this to be, then the approach I wish to support rejects such an extreme position. But the opposite position of "objectivism," according to which whatever value, meaning, or importance there is, is due entirely to what is found or discovered as already inherent in some object, other person, and situation to which the meaning, value, or importance is assigned, is equally unacceptable. We are not called upon to choose one alternative or the other, because *both* poles of an interactive relation are *always* involved in various ways: the individual human existent(s) on the one hand, and the objects or circumstances with which the human existent interacts on the other. It is as a result of this interaction between the jointly present participants that the human existent(s) involved find or share in creating some type or degree of meaning in that interaction. The resultant meaning, whatever it is, arises from properties and contributions made by, and from, both sides of the interactive relation. The meaning, as it were, exists "in between" their mutual interaction. We could say the meaning exists *for* the human existents involved and also *depends on* and *is about* the materials or features of the existents, occasions, and circumstances that brought the interaction into play.

As we go on to examine the various factors that play their special roles in filling out our basic schema of human interactions, it will become increasingly obvious that we cannot examine any one of the three factors (human existents, interactions as the carriers of meanings, and other existents) without involving the other two; the three factors are interdependent. Let us consider some simple examples.

A person sits in a chair. An infant is picked up and held securely by its mother. A woman weighs herself on a scale and finds (to her delight) she has lost five pounds. An aviator parachutes to safety. A tourist climbs the Leaning Tower of Pisa. An astronaut walks on the Moon. While in a rapidly ascending elevator, a person experiences his insides "falling." An astronaut while in orbit takes a "space walk."

Consider next the following set of interactive human experiences. An infant sucks at its mother's breast. A person in a coma is fed intravenously. On a visit to Paris, someone eats *escargots* for the first time. Lost in the desert, parched, and "near death," a person comes upon an oasis. In a hurry, an individual "grabs a sandwich" at a fast-food restaurant. A person attends a golden wedding anniversary party for his or her parents. A Nobel Prize winner is feted at a special dinner.

In the first set, despite their wide-ranging differences, the underlying, common feature involves the physical phenomenon of *gravity;* in the second set, the underlying, common feature is the presence of the biological activity of *feeding.* In each of the foregoing sets of examples of interactive human existents, there are nevertheless wide variations that affect the question of determining the "meaning" of the interaction for the human existent(s) involved.

It will be evident on examining any one of the foregoing examples that, in addition to what was called "the underlying common factor," a determination of the "meaning" for the individual in a particular case calls for consideration of a great number of factors. Among the latter is the kind or degree of conscious awareness present; the relatively trivial, commonplace character of the interaction; or, on the contrary, its being highly charged emotionally and memorable in a strong sense. In the case of the mother picking up and holding her infant securely in her arms, the degree of awareness or of the simplicity or complexity in the type of feeling involved is surely different in character for the two participants at the time of the interaction. The perspective of the meaning of the event for the parents at their anniversary party is bound to be in part different from that of a participating child or grandchild. The purely physical (gravitational) interaction of a person sitting in a chair may have a different meaning depending, for example, upon whether it occurs because the person is tired, is being operated on by a dentist, is attending a concert, or is waiting to be seen for an important job interview, etc. Some of these examples of interactions may be commonplace and of a recurrent nature for a given individual (e.g., "grabbing a sandwich" at a fast food restaurant, the feeling in one's insides while ascending rapidly in an elevator, weighing oneself on a scale), while others may be highly unusual, infrequent, or "unique" (e.g., taking a space walk, being guest of honor at a Nobel Prize dinner, and so on.

If one were to undertake to widen the range of examples, contexts, and occasions in which interactions between human existents and other existents provide meanings for the human participants, the project would not only be formidable but interminable. For there is no single list or classification that would, in any universally acceptable way, be available for such purposes. One can traverse and crisscross the field of human interactions along innumerable paths, some of which, no doubt, would be more fruitful and enlightening than others.

In determining the locus of meaning in an interaction involving human existents, the situation that calls for more detailed examination bears a certain limited resemblance to the situation involved in examining the application of grammatical rules (in Wittgenstein's sense) in the case of understanding the role of language in human experience. In the case of grammatical rules that govern the varied uses of language and concepts, it belongs to a prerogative of human autonomy to determine their construction, adoption, and sanction. There is nothing "in reality" to which one can appeal to decide which of various rules one does or can adopt is "true," since, taken apart from their applications, all rules are devoid of truth or falsity. The advantages (including truth) to be found in the use of one or another set of conventionally adopted rules or "ways of thinking" embodied in a language, lies in the *application* of the rules or ways of thinking to actual circumstances encountered in experience. Those circumstances—for example, as reported in the observational data obtained in a laboratory—are found by consulting something that is determined apart from the sphere of human autonomy; this independent element is not invented or totally controlled by human beings. Thus, having adopted, say, the metric system of rules for measuring lengths, and conveying the results obtained in a particular case of carrying out a measurement by means of the use of that language, whether one is to say that a measured object is four meters long is not determined exclusively by the language system employed. The actual length is found by certain procedures and observations; it is not invented or arbitrarily constructed. In short, in the case of man-made languages, the outcome of the application of those languages in particular circumstances is a matter of the conjoint operation of language and the subject matter to which it is applied. Both are necessary; neither by itself is sufficient.

The same general distinction between inherited or accepted conditions and their possible uses or applications in particular circumstances that holds in understanding the operation of languages is also useful by way of general analogy in assigning the role of different factors that make for the presence of meanings in the broader sphere of interactive relations of human existents with other existents. A particular human existent brings a fund of personal experience along with certain pre-established or inherited mechanisms, rules, propensities, preferences, and ways of thinking. These are the deposit of biologically inherited (genetic) factors, or of cultural, family, and educational influences, along with the funding of previous personal experiences and habits, the unreflective expression of spontaneous impulses or, in still other cases, the outcome of fresh, deliberated choice. All of these—however conditioned, naturally determined, or consciously arrived at by the human participants—color and affect the resultant meaning of a given interaction. The result of the interaction—its *meaning* for the human participants—is the joint product of the meeting, mingling, and "application" of what all the existents involved in an interaction bring to its occurrence.

The analogy between the language situation and the human interaction situation, accordingly, is this. Whereas, on the one hand, in the case of the language situation (where, we shall assume, for purposes of illustration, an interest is predominantly cognitive, as it is in science), the *application* of inherited or accepted grammatical rules to the data of observation results in judgments of *truth* or *falsity* with respect to such applications, in the case, on the other hand, of interactions between human existents and other existents, the "application" of inherited or given conditions in an interaction results in some form or degree of *meaning* (*import*-ance), rather than one of "truth or falsity," for the human participants.

In support of making use of the notion of "degree of meaning (value, *import*-ance)" belonging to any instance of an interactive relation between a human existent and other existents, it will be helpful to make use of the metaphor of *meaning-charge*. The sense of "charge" I shall employ in the phrase "meaning-charge" is borrowed by way of analogy from its use in electrical physics. The basic distinction between positive and negative charges as used in connection with electrical phenomena can be extended through suitable modifications and extensions to the case of meaning. Thus one may begin by drawing a fundamental distinction between those meaning-charges that are positive or negative as well as those that are neutral. However, instead of thinking of a "charge" (as in the case of electricity) as a property inherent in, or carried by one or another of the electrically charged participants in an interacting electrical relation, we shall think of the *meaning-charge* as coming into existence and located in the *interaction-relation* itself.

This rough, threefold distinction among meaning-charges (as positive, negative, or neutral) can play its role not only in a great variety of interactive circumstances and contexts—for example, where one recognizes the advantage of identifying the predominant meaning of an interaction as either cognitive or affective—but also one or another of the types of meaning-charge may be assigned to a relatively simple or brief interaction or, on the other hand, by way of summing up the overall residual quality of a temporally extended or complicated interaction. On receiving a letter, one may find it gives highly welcome news (for example, admission to a college of one's choice), or, contrariwise, unwelcome information or depressing news (for example, being advised of dismissal from one's job), while the contents of still other letters yield no discernible meaning-charge. The latter are a matter of total indifference (for example, most "junk mail"). Similar distinctions among positive, negative, or neutral meaning-charges are easily found in many other interactions: e.g., on meeting a number of people for the first time, visiting different areas of a city, taking particular courses in college, walking through the galleries of a museum, and so on.

Normally, however, we may not rest content with making simple classifications of positive or negative meaning-charge, but are interested in (or requested to) draw distinctions of a rough quantitative sort ("very much," "very little," "a moderate amount"). One says: "Glen Gould's performance of Bach's *Well-Tempered Clavier* is by far more satisfying musically in making the structure clear and giving me more auditory pleasure (in present terminology, has greater positive meaning-charge for me) than any other reading or interpretation I have ever heard."

Relatively simple models for the production of meaning-charge are: a tennis match, climbing a mountain, planting a garden, or the patterned and carefully controlled interchanges among the members of a team of jugglers. In any interaction, simple or complex, of relatively short duration or extending over a considerable stretch of time, involving only few existents or many, the meaning-charge of the interaction among the existents—its intensity, memorability, and impact on lives affected—is the product of the contributions of human and nonhuman factors, agents, and conditions. When we consider the temporal extent of an interaction between an individual human existent and other existents, the character of the meaning-charge will be affected by possible changes over a period of time (long or short) on either or both side(s) of the interactive relation. The quality of meaning-charge experienced by the individuals involved in a friendship or marriage may change over the years in various ways—growing in intensity in one direction, undergoing ups and downs, or perhaps dissolving into neutrality and indifference altogether. The same may be true of one's approval, disapproval, or relative indifference with respect to one's views of a political party or the officeholders in a particular administration.

Changes at either end, too, in the participants of a specific interactive connection, may determine the resultant quality or degree of its meaning-charge. Every performer or teacher knows that even though, say, the performance or lecture was presented "in the same way" on two separate occassions to different audiences, the results may be widely different. And, of course, the changes may occur for a variety of reasons: for example, the performer may have developed a more profound understanding of the material, or, in the other direction, the performer may have grown stale, tired, psychologically troubled, or physically ill; the opportunities for frequent contact between individuals become fewer or virtually nonexistent because of physical separation, poor health, dropping of memberships and interchanges in common organizations and activities, and so on. In short, the quality and degree of meaning-charge in particular interactions may be relatively stable or undergo radical transformations; they are sensitive functions of the several relevant underlying factors present in an interaction.

Having made the foregoing distinctions of types of meaning-charge (positive, negative, neutral, as well as those which involve differences of degree or amount with respect each of these), it is important to consider to what extent, if at all, an acceptance of this way of thinking about meanings as having charges agrees with the way in which the terms "meaning," "meaningful," "meaningless" (or "absurd") are commonly used in describing the character of human life.

According to ordinary usage, the terms "meaning" and "meaningful" would be understood, at best, as applying only to those experiences which are positive from the point of view of the classification offered by the meaning-charge approach. If an experience is deemed absurd or meaningless, this would imply—contrary to the view of the meaning-charge approach—that it is *not* to be included at all within the range of life-experiences that have meaning or are meaningful. On the other hand, on the scheme here proposed, the term "meaning" (as used to describe the character of a consciously recognized interaction between a human existent and other existents) can be either negative, positive, or neutral. In acknowledgment of this discrepancy concerning the use of the term "meaning," it is clear that what is at stake, at a minimum, is a terminological matter. There is no right or wrong in these different choices that can be settled by appeal to some independent reality. Each represents a stipulation or convention, and the important issues have to do with what gains or advantages there are in the application of either scheme. Nevertheless there are advantages in the use of the wide framework offered by the notion of meaning-charge that are not easily accommodated or given any illumination by the conventional use of the terms "meaningful" or "meaningless." Among other benefits, the proposal to consider negative or neutral meanings (along with positive ones) under the rubric of "meaning(s)" provides a wider latitude for the use of this expression than does the usage that restricts its use to only those meaning-charges that are positive. The more inclusive range made available by the meaning-charge approach for identifying meanings of various sorts allows for taking all of these into account, whatever their character, in reviewing and summing up the values achieved in a particular life.

One may think of the life of an individual human existent as consisting of a complex series and interweaving of interactions in which the individual participates between the limits of birth and death. In examining the question of what could be said about the meaning of a person's life, we do well to pluralize the treatment of "meaning." The meanings found in any life are associated with the great multitude of interactions that compose a particular life. However, there is no *unique* way of identifying or listing the interactions that compose a person's life. Individual interactions do not come prepackaged and labeled as such. A life can be "cut up" into its individual interactions in various ways, depending on the coordinates or parameters chosen, and on what the person judges is important in his or her life. Moreover, not only is there no uniquely correct way of identifying *an* individual interaction, but this is also the case in marking out in a given life (for purposes of review) what should be included as the meanings associated with the interactions belonging to certain selected periods or activities in one's life. Each of these, too, when blocked out, collects a variety of examples, whether trivial, routine, or momentous. If one should undertake to survey the meanings associated with the multitude of interactions in any such segment—to sum up the overall quality of those meanings—once again there is no uniquely correct way in which this can be accomplished, nor done once and for all.

Every life of every individual existent is its own unique composite of all the meanings it accumulates and brings to light in the course of its passage from birth to death. Each meaning in each interaction has its own meaning-charge (positive, negative, neutral); its own place in a period, segment, or aspect of the person's life. Since each and every life is the setting and carrier of its own accumulated meanings, and since each review of a life, or the continual undergoing of its own interactions, is unique to each individual existent's life, the profile of meanings for one person's life cannot be duplicated in every respect by any other. The world-line of every individual existent, encased in its own network and sheathing of meanings, is a different world-line from any other, however much it may, in certain respects, parallel other world-lines or intersect with them at certain junctures. Some are short, some longer; some are rich in the diversity of their meanings, while others are lean or restricted in what life made possible for them; some possess a profusion of positive meaning-charges, while others are dominated by negative ones; some parts of the life of some persons are creative, while others are noticeably deficient or lacking in this respect; some meanings are morally praiseworthy, while others are open to condemnation, and still others are morally neutral. When we take all this into account, it should make it all the more obvious how entirely vacuous and futile it is to indulge in the kind of generalization that consists in saying *all* life, i.e., the life of each and every human existent, is meaningful or meaningless.

LIFE UNDER THE ASPECT OF BOUNDLESS EXISTENCE

Cosmic Spirituality

Our discussion thus far has focussed on the way in which meanings in life are associated with the ways in which human existents, as parts of the existent universe, interact with other existents. For most persons, the bulk of attention and concern in their daily round of activities is devoted to earning a living; to carrying out one's role in family life; to various other modes of social involvement; and to satisfying biological, intellectual, esthetic, or professional interests. In short, for the vast majority of human existents, the bulk of attention and concern is centered on other particular existents, whether animate or inanimate, whether human or not, whether found in nature or culturally encountered, appropriated, inherited, or added to by the transformative and creative contributions of the individual. Whatever meaning life has for a particular individual is to be found in the character of the multiple meanings that make up that life—their distribution and their interrelationships with one another, together with the way they are experienced, judged, and valued with respect to their meaning-charge.

If one accepts the distinction between the existent universe and Boundless Existence as drawn by the world picture I have sketched, then it is part of that acceptance to recognize that Boundless Existence is neither an existent, a collection of existents, nor even the supposed totality of existents. Since it is not an existent, Boundless Existence cannot act on us, nor can a human existent *interact* with it. Since, too, it is not an existent in the way in which the observable universe or any of its parts is, it cannot be explored, modified, perceived, investigated, or understood.

Moreover, it is a fundamental dimension of Reality, and as such is not only to be accorded equal status with other fundamental principles on an ontological level of the world picture we are exploring, but should also receive full and equal attention in a philosophy of life that purports to serve as a schema for envisioning our place in Reality, i.e., as a guide for our actions and as a way of judging the possible values of life.

As far as we know, it is exclusively given to human existents not only to interact with and progressively understand other existents, but to become increasingly aware of Boundless Existence. To bring Boundless Existence into intensified awareness and to let its presence permeate and affect all our interactions with other existents, is, however, for the vast majority of human existents, a relatively rare achievement and practice. Whatever benefits such awareness could bring, is, therefore, absent from the lives of most human existents or the dominant philosophies by which they are guided.

As contrasted with the way in which our lives can be viewed insofar as we are engaged in interacting with other existents, the question of the meaning of life when viewed under the aspect of Boundless Existence is precisely what we shall be interested in examining. When realized to a sufficient degree, we shall find that an intensified awareness of Boundless Existence could play a crucial role in influencing our view of life as situated both "in" the universe and "in" Boundless Existence.

A guiding presupposition in our efforts toward formulating a workable and acceptable philosophy of life is the claim that the awareness of Boundless Existence has a special role to play in satisfying the need for cultivating a form of cosmic spirituality. If this thesis is to be upheld, however, we should need to answer the following queries.

In the first place, we seem to be faced with a dilemma arising from a possible ambiguity in the very use of the phrase "cosmic spirituality." If it means that we are, in some way, to look to the existent universe to give us the guidelines for the cultivation and practice of a spiritual dimension to our lives, then, on the basis of the analysis we have offered thus far of how to regard the use of the term "universe" according to the expanding-horizons approach, we should be ill-advised to look to the universe to provide such guidelines. At best, where attained, scientific intelligibility of the universe is the empirically tested product of human conceptual construal, and is of course, as such, a human achievement or good. Nevertheless, we should surely want to acknowledge that it is not the only good to be found in life, nor a sufficient basis for determining the selection, guidance, and pursuit of all other modes of experience and human activity that might in their own individual ways also yield genuine value. While scientific intelligibility, as achieved on a cosmological level, may be recognized to play a significant role in the attainment of an outlook of cosmic spirituality, it surely should not be expected to exhaustively define and constitute the nature of such spirituality.

From a broad ontological point of view, the only other direction of cosmic scope to which we can turn is Boundless Existence. However, since a recognition of Boundless Existence is tantamount to an awareness of the absence of any sort of intelligibility in the ontological fact that the universe Exists, it would seem to follow that we cannot look to this dimension of Reality, either, to provide guidance in selecting and pursuing sources of positively charged interactive meanings in our lives. How, then, can our participating "in" Boundless Existence contribute to a sense of the meaning of life beyond those meanings found, established, undergone, or enjoyed in interacting with ordinary existents?

In light of the apparent futility in finding genuine spiritual guidance by looking to either of the two foregoing major cosmic directions—as a target for scientific understanding or as the ontological locus for becoming aware of Boundless Existence—in what does the supposed advantage of cultivating an attitude of cosmic spirituality consist? Why, indeed, use the expression "*cosmic* spirituality" at all? Is it not misleading to do so?

Furthermore, there would appear to be another difficulty or paradox in the effort to include an awareness of Boundless Existence among the positive values or goods of life. Since it is devoid of all properties, Boundless Existence is another way of interpreting and sanctioning the use of the concept of "Nothing." Yet how can the admission of such Nothing into our lives perform a crucial and important role? How should we make room for it in our manifold interactions with various Somethings? Would it not be paradoxical to say that the awareness of Boundless Existence is also a meaning of some kind? How can our awareness of it be the source for achieving meaning, if (as we have argued earlier) meanings are to be found only in the interactions of human existents with other existents? We seem to be caught in the dilemma of being drawn both to including and to excluding it from the domain of meanings in life. Is there some way of overcoming this dilemma and resolving the paradox?

First, a terminological remark. I have previously used the terms "meaning," "value," and "importance" in connection with the sphere of human interactions with other existents. In this context and under this restriction, I gave special prominence, in particular, to the use of the expression "meaning" in its plural form. We face now an important question. Shall we say that the awareness of Boundless Existence is to be reckoned among the meanings of life; that it, too, has, or can have, a special type of value or importance?

The question calls for a terminological decision. One possibility is to continue with our earlier usage and restrict the use of the terms "value," "importance," and "meaning" to what is present only in those cases that involve the conscious interactions between human existents and other existents. For reasons already given concerning the special character of the nature of Boundless Existence, and as contrasted with the typical sources and types of interactive meanings, a thorough appreciation of the special character of our awareness of Boundless Existence would seem to give us good grounds for rejecting the suggestion that we classify it under the same heading—"meanings"—as those involving the interaction between existents. This restriction and exclusion could have its benefits: it would remind us of the gulf that separates Boundless Existence from the ontological status of existents, as well as the difference between an awareness of Boundless Existence and our normal interactions with existents in the universe.

However, there is an opposing line of thought that inclines us in another direction and points to a different decision. The awareness of Boundless Existence is, after all, one mode or level of human experience, and when seen not only in terms of its intrinsic character, but also in terms of the possible consequences it can have for the rest of our experience, it would seem wholly arbitrary to exclude it from the range of human experiences that can be credited with being a source of meaning, value, or importance in our lives. In the light of this consideration, and provided we can show the gounds for its inclusion, the decision to make room for this experience in an appropriate way is therefore marked by a readiness to extend the range of possible application of the terms "value," "importance," and "meaning" so that they could encompass the awareness of Boundless Existence. To be sure, this latter course could only be warranted if we were to agree to keep in mind and stress the differences between the kinds of meanings or values found in interactions with other existents and the meaning or value that attaches to the awareness of Boundless Existence. In light of the foregoing reminder, and in full agreement with the need to keep the aforementioned proviso in mind, I shall, in what follows, adopt and implement the second option.

Wonder

The human capacity for wonder is aroused by different stimuli and takes various forms. One aspect of being aroused to a state of wonder is its affective quality: the feeling of being overwhelmed, astounded, and emotionally stirred, sometimes to an intense degree. When present, the feeling of wonder is also frequently accompanied by verbal expressions of an exclamatory or interrogative character. Various familiar occasions and kinds of experience that give rise to a feeling of wonder and to its expression in language are the following: we marvel at an outstanding example of human virtuosity; at an altogether unexpected, novel natural phenomenon; or at an event whose occurrence we find totally baffling and unexplained. Typical occasions and stimuli for arousing our sense of wonder belong to the sphere of human virtuosity. "How is it possible," we exclaim, "that this can be done by any human being(s)?" We are apt to say this sort of thing while enjoying the fruits of extreme musical creativity by a Mozart or Bach, in witnessing the performance of highly complicated acrobatic acts, or in beholding the arrangement of megaliths on Easter Island or at Stonehenge. Again, some wholly unfamiliar natural occurrence—for example, a solar eclipse or the flareup of a supernova encountered for the first time at a particular stage of human history and knowledge—may also evoke our exclamations of wonderment and questions conveying our sense of puzzlement.

The asking of these questions may eventually lead to answers that come to be accepted. Satisfactory explanations may become available concerning the purpose and techniques used in erecting the structure at Stonehenge, the physics underlying solar eclipses or explosions of supernovas, the kinds of training practices and skills that make possible the virtuoso performances of a complicated acrobatic act. These explanations may lead, in some cases, to a lessening or even an evaporation of the degree of our initial sense of wonder. In other cases, however, the feeling of wonderment may persist even in the face of accepted explanations. In still other cases, no satisfactory explanation or scientific understanding may be forthcoming: one is left both the feeling of wonderment and a fund of unanswered questions. Can one explain Mozart's creativity?

Thus far the examples I have mentioned, taken from the sphere of natural events or human performances, belong to the domain of *existents*. We wonder how or why some particular occurrence, object, construction, or phenomenon can exist. With respect to such existents, we are inclined to believe that what is still unexplained will, in time and with persistent inquiry, yield to understanding: we believe they are in principle intelligible, even though not all of them have as yet so yielded.

There is, however, another side of human wonderment more germane to our present interest. The intensified awareness of the dimension of Reality I have labeled "Boundless Existence" is made possible by cultivating one direction of exercise of this capacity. Here, too, when cultivated or isolated for special attention, the wonderment aroused by Boundless Existence involves an affective response, a feeling or emotion that for some persons may be (or become) quite intense. Yet it is different from the feelings provoked by other wondrous occasions and stimuli. It is not directed at some particular human construction or performance, at some object, phenomenon, or occurrence encountered or undergone in experience. Boundless Existence is not an object, not a human creation or performance, not a natural phenomenon. It is simply the ontologically fundamental fact that the universe Exists.

Of course, aside from its unique affective quality, what further distinguishes this experience is that should we attempt (as many have done!) to convey our wonderment by means of a question such as "Why?" or "How?" to explain the Existence of the universe, we cannot go on—at least according to the world picture I am here engaged in articulating—to satisfactorily answer such questions. Boundless Existence is and remains wholly unintelligible. It defies and defeats all efforts at providing satisfactory explanations that would provide reasons, grounds, conditions, causes, or motives. All that we are left with, as far as wonderment goes, is an altogether unique affective quality.

We might be tempted to express the difference between our responses of wonderment in the face of various special kinds of existents in the universe on the one hand, and in becoming aware of the sheer Existence of the universe on the other, by saying that the former are meaningful in one way or another, whereas the Existence of the universe (Boundless Existence) is utterly meaningless. To this, however, an immediate objection might be forthcoming. Would not the characterization of Boundless Existence as being "utterly meaningless" conflict with our earlier-stated readiness to include the recognition of Boundless Existence within the (extended) range of meanings in human experience? The answer to this challenge is to be found in drawing a fundamental distinction between the way the term "meaningless" could be used when applied to Boundless Existence and the way it is used in ordinary contexts.

What makes it possible for existents to be meaningful is their having properties and powers of one sort or another. Meanings are found as the result of the interaction of conscious human existents with other existents (including other human existents). Both the human existent on one side of the interactive link and the existent on the other side with which one is interacting have their own powers and capacities, their own properties. It is as a result of the interaction of these properties *on both sides of the interactive bridge* that meaningfulness for the human existent(s) arises. It is not the human existent alone, on one side, that brings the meaning into existence. That with which one is interacting contributes its own share: it manifests its own powers and capacities. I lift a rock and find it distressingly heavy. It is not simply the powers and limits of my body's frame and musculature that produces this outcome, but the fact, too, that the rock has a certain mass and weight in the Earth's gravitational field and contributes the effects of these properties to the total experience as felt (meaningfully) at the human end of the transaction.

An existent—whatever its size, location, complexity, rarity, or duration—can be said to be meaningful for a human existent insofar as its occurrence or presence makes a difference and becomes a matter of interest in some way or degree for the human existent encountering and interacting with it.

Such meaningfulness or interest can take the form of wanting, at the least, to satisfy our curiosity or desire to understand its presence or occurrence. In the case of meaningful human interactions with other existents that have as their principal outcome the achievement of understanding by the human knower at one end, there is a bipolar interaction involving relevant contributions from both sides of the interactive bridge. By virtue of the power of creating and using languages of various sorts and the conceptual creativity manifested in such activity, the tested application of such conceptual powers brought to bear on the observational materials furnished from the side of the existents to which those conceptual ventures are addressed, becomes a source of meaningfulness for an inquiring and thoughtful human existent.

In addition to provoking human cognitive interests, existents may, of course, also pose other reasons for our concern or interest in interacting with them. They may arouse esthetic, economic, sexual, sentimental, technologic, and a host of other special types of interest. Our interactions with other existents are meaningful insofar as one or a combination of human capacities and interests that they engage and activate may make a difference in our lives—momentarily or over a stretch of time, in a relatively isolated way or in interrelation with various other activities and pursuits. The meaningfulness of an existent for us may be restricted to its intelligibility—its being understood in causal or other terms—like understanding why the stars shine. In other cases, the meaningfulness of an existent may consist in its affording some satisfaction of one sort or another, even if one does not understand it in causal terms or as the outcome of a deliberate act or production by a conscious agent. Of course there are countless examples of existents deemed meaningful because their origin, structure, and operation already are (or can become) both intelligible and also valuable for additional reasons—like appreciating the uses of a clock, a radio, or a vacuum cleaner.

If we say that something is meaningless as far as we are concerned, it is because we neither understand its occurrence nor does it have any other value or interest for us: its meaning-charge is altogether neutral. However, despite the judgment that someone may pass as to the meaninglessness of an event, performance, or phenomenon, this judgment is *not irrevocable*. One's curiosity to understand may be aroused, the possible benefits and uses that something may have for the individual, hitherto bypassed and ignored, may suddenly loom into importance and motivate a genuine interest: what was previously meaningless becomes to some degree meaningful and possessed of positive meaning-charge. The occurrence of some natural event and phenomenon or the presence and actions of some other human being(s) activate relevant responses by the aroused person.

None of the foregoing types of conditions for achieving meaningfulness in our experience are available in the case of becoming aware of Boundless Existence. Unlike any example of meaningfulness found in connection with existents, the ontological dimension of Boundless Existence is devoid of any form of meaningfulness. It has no properties or capacities of its own that, were such present, could be brought into operation with ourselves. It is not observable, hence not intelligible in a testable way as is the case with existents. It is not even valuable in manifesting certain powers and capacities that, when brought into interactive relation with our own preferences, habits, and sensitivities, produce results that *we* find charged with meaning and value of one sort or another as the outcome of the mingling of our contribution and that from its own side.

At best, all we can have is an *awareness* of Boundless Existence. But this awareness is not an exercise in understanding, of making possible a kind of intelligibility. Nor is it a case of our finding some value in our awareness of Boundless Existence because of the presence and activation of certain properties or powers *it* possesses. The only contribution to the resultant experience of awareness is made from our human side. It is the combination of this absence of all normal conditions and sources of meaningfulness (such as we find in the case of our interactions with existents) that distinguishes our experience of Boundless Existence from all other human experiences.

Although Boundless Existence is not an existent, the awareness of it is a result of our responding to the fact that the universe Exists. It is in the human response to this latter vertical dimension of Reality that it becomes a meaning for us. The altogether unique aspect of this meaning is that, when considered with respect to the coordinates of meaning-charge and the distinction between cognitive and affective meanings, it has two altogether unique features. With respect to the cognitive coordinate, it lies at the very bottom of the *negative* side of meaning-charge: it is neither perceived, understood, nor imagined. On the other hand, with respect to the coordinate of affective-meanings, it is at the very limit of the *positive* direction with respect to what can arouse wonder. It is not only utterly unintelligible, but for that very reason generates an even greater amount of wonder than any other actual or possible stimulus. However wondrous any other existent might be, it at least is open to some actual or possible understanding! Not so, however, for Boundless Existence. It is "wholly other" both on a cognitive scale of unintelligibility as well as on a scale of affective-meanings in the degree to which it provokes wonderment. It transcends everything else that might be measured on either scale.

Having reached this point, I propose to investigate the way in which our awareness of Boundless Existence can have important consequences. "Consequences?" one asks. "How can that which has no properties or powers have consequences? Put me in a room with insufficient oxygen and I will suffer the consequences. Let me be exposed to the thoughts of a great teacher or writer and my own thoughts will show the consequences of that exposure. And so on. But how can Boundless Existence have any impact on my life?"

Consequences

The answer, of course, immediately follows from what has already been said. It is not Boundless Existence that has any direct or indirect impact on an individual life, since it does not have any properties: it cannot act on a human existent any more than a person can act on it. Human existents cannot *interact* with Boundless Existence— nor, of course, can any other types of existents. Rather, what does or can have consequences for the life of a human existent is an *awareness* of Boundless Existence, not Boundless Existence itself.

In chapter 1, when canvassing the variety of incentives for raising the question of the meaning of life, I pointed out something of the variety of those incentives and occasions. I should not want to maintain that the intensified awareness of Boundless Existence can play a central role for all who raise the question, regardless of the situations or circumstances in which it is raised. It may play such a role for some persons, but it need not do so for all. It does become relevant and important for a person who is open to considerations of a cosmological or ontological scope and could benefit from seeing the question about the meaning of life in this broader context. It is with these circumstances and for such persons that the introduction of an awareness of Boundless Existence might help to resolve the pressures that led to the raising of the question. It is within the framework of this subclass of "big-picture" incentives that the following discussion is primarily located.

All fundamental principles in *any* world picture have consequences in the actions, attitudes, and other beliefs held by the person who accepts the given world picture: world pictures permeate the life of a human existent. They are intertwined with all particular aspects and engagements of a person's life; their unquestioned acceptance makes a difference in the life of the individual. In this respect, the world picture that includes among its fundamental principles the recognition of Boundless Existence is no different from any other world picture. The recognition of Boundless Existence as a basic dimension of Reality plays its own distinctive role in influencing the attitudes, feelings, beliefs, and course of action for the person for whom that recognition is sufficiently developed, unquestioned, and securely established, just as the special and distinctive fundamental principles that belong to a different world picture guide and affect the day-to-day life of those who adhere to them.

In examining the distinctive role that the awareness of Boundless Existence has, it is important not only to bear in mind how the expression "Boundless Existence" is here used to identify part of the world picture I am engaged in expounding, but also not to be misled by the intrusion of assignments to the use of this expression that are influenced by wrong associations or supposed analogies that only serve to distort its genuine use and correct understanding.

The awareness of Boundless Existence consists in dwelling on the basic fact that Boundless Existence is totally without properties, that it is utterly unintelligible, that it lacks any materials or powers of its own, that it does not have any concern or interest of one sort or another, conscious or otherwise, that might affect positively or negatively, or contribute in any way to, the character and achievability of various types of meanings in the lives of human existents. The consequences for our lives are the consequences of having this awareness of the unique "character" of Boundless Existence—the fact that it has no character or properties of its own! It is this realization that is of great *import*-ance to us.

The role of an awareness of Boundless Existence in the cultivation of cosmic spirituality is not to offer a route of disengagement from the multiple interactive meanings of a person's life and withdrawal (escape) into a focused, exclusive, meditative absorption into the wholly featureless character of Boundless Existence. It is, on the contrary, to let an intensified awareness of the characterlessness of Boundless Existence (its "emptiness") permeate and serve as a *co-present* background for the foreground of involvement in one or another (or combination of) ongoing interactive meanings in the life of a person.[29]

---

29. The Zen Patriarch Hui-Neng wrote: "The capacity of mind is broad and huge, like the vast sky. Do not sit with a mind fixed on emptiness. If you do you will fall into a neutral kind of emptiness. Emptiness includes the sun, moon, stars, and planets, the great earth, mountains and rivers, all trees and grasses, bad men and good men, bad things and good things, heaven and hell; they are all in the midst of emptiness. The emptiness of human nature is also like this." (*Tan-ching*, 24, translated by P. B. Yampolsky: *The Platform Sutra of the Sixth Patriarch* [New York: Columbia University Press, 1967]).

Since interactive meanings range in degrees and types of meaning-charge as realized in the particular life span (or segment of a life span) of an individual life, the awareness of Boundless Existence as a silent, accompanying witness and commentator to all such interactive meanings, can perform a positive role of its own in qualifying, in important ways, our attitudes toward the having of such interactive meanings—whether the latter be positive, negative, or neutral in their meaning-charge. The awareness of Boundless Existence is not a detached, self-sufficient, experience of its own; it is, rather, a silent partner accompanying and intermingled with the experience of this or that interactive meaning. The awareness of Boundless Existence is the vertical dimension in a life characterized by cosmic spirituality that accompanies the plotting (that is, the *living*) of that life on a horizontal dimension, where the latter ranges over all interactive meanings. The vertical dimension in a spiritual life is not a *replacement* for the horizontal dimension, any more than in geometry a second coordinate (say, the *y* coordinate) for mapping the locus of a point, line, or figure is a replacement for the role of the first dimension (the *x* coordinate): it is an *addition* or *supplement* to the use of the other dimension in such mapping.

The important question, of course, is what benefits to a person's life the exercise of such an additional vertical dimension to cosmic spirituality makes possible. What does it bring to the life-space of meanings in a person's life that would be absent if that life were lived altogether on a horizontal dimension of interactive meanings? The intriguing and crucial question that needs answering is how, if Boundless Existence is Nothing and therefore lacking in all qualities of its own, the presence of an awareness of this Nothing can contribute to our experiences of one or another Something within the sphere of interactive meanings during the course of a life.

One immediate, sound answer—though fraught with opportunities for misunderstanding—is to say that by "taking the viewpoint" of Boundless Existence with respect to the interactive meanings of life, one adopts a radically different stance from that which is present in being immersed in the experience of any of those interactive meanings. The immediate and valid objection to this way of expressing the matter is that, if Boundless Existence is lacking in all properties of its own, it cannot offer a position or foothold from whose viewpoint (when assumed or taken on as one's own) one can then look at our normal life of activities and meanings. Boundless Existence has no stance or viewpoint of its own, and therefore it cannot (even temporarily or for the benefit of the exercise) be shared by us.

It would also be equally unsatisfactory to say that by adopting the viewpoint of Boundless Existence one is exchanging our normal subjective viewpoint for one that is objective. The terms "subjective" and "objective" are wholly inappropriate here. For a so-called objective viewpoint is still a viewpoint or stance adopted from the position of someone who calls on and manifests certain properties, abilities, and interests, even though these may be, admittedly, different in certain crucial respects from those found in a subjective point of view. We say a scientist, who has cultivated and assumed a position of neutral objectivity—say a student of social phenomena such as strikes, revolutions, terrorist activities, or political parties—is expected to be different from those actually participating in them and who have a passionate interest in one side or another of the conflicts involved. Or again, a surgeon operating on his patient is expected to have a different, wholly objective approach to the nature and outcome of the operation he or she performs from that of the patient undergoing the operation or those emotionally close to the patient. Yet the objective point of view, here illustrated, is, of course, determined by certain special interests, capacities, and powers of a professional or scientific sort, although these are of a different kind from those exhibiting purely subjective, personal interests. Since Boundless Existence has no properties whatsoever, it has neither objective nor subjective interests nor any point of view at all. Hence one cannot presume to identify with and assume the particular supposedly objective viewpoint possessed by Boundless Existence itself.

A more satisfactory way of making the point intended by recommending that we take the viewpoint of Boundless Existence is to say that, in being aware of Boundless Existence and its emptiness, it is we, by virtue of this awareness, who can look at our own lives in a different way from that which we normally bring to bear when we are involved in our daily activities and the interactive meanings they yield. Our viewpoint, although different, is still a human one—if you wish, still a subjective one—because it is made by a human subject. However, if all viewpoints are subjective in this sense, then even objective ones or those made from the vantage point of an awareness of Boundless Existence are also subjective, and the term "subjective" loses its normal usefulness as a term of contrast with those that are not subjective.

What, then, is the special benefit to our lives that an awareness of Boundless Existence has? If, as human existents aware of Boundless Existence, we were to learn to take the latter dimension into account in considering the full range of possible meaningful experiences (those that are interactive as well as, in the present instance, those that are not interactive), what does it add to our experience that would not otherwise be present? What *difference* does the presence of this awareness make? In particular, what does an intensified awareness of Boundless Existence contribute to answering the question about "the meaning of life" and in helping to characterize the nature of cosmic spirituality—the two related themes that have been at the center of our interest in this book?

One of these consequences is that we are saved from falling prey to, and being influenced by, misleading accounts of the nature of human existence. Human beings are prone to succumb to the power of such misleading accounts since, in many cases, their acceptance feeds on underlying human emotions of various sorts—fear, despair, anxiety, hope, trustingness, and so on—as these are projected from their normally limited human contexts and occasions of expression involving the interactions of human existents with other particular existents, onto generalizations about the (alleged) nature of the universe or reality "as a whole." In the face of the allegedly inescapable dominance of suffering and pain in life, some religiously inspired philosophies of life counsel a withdrawal from and attenuation of life by stressing in general a meditative absorption in and mystical contemplation of emptiness (*sunyata*) that marks the achievement of Nirvana.

At the same time, the orientation provided by awareness of the characterlessness of Boundless Existence also separates itself from a blind optimistic faith in the supposedly fundamental, overall goodness and long-range beneficence of God or reality, such as one finds in some traditional theistic philosophies, as well as in those of a neo-Platonic variety. Such optimistic faith is found, for example, in religious viewpoints that have a conception of personal immortality and an afterlife, according to which the reward of eternal happiness in Heaven awaits those who earned such reward by deeds done in "this world."

The misleading result of such projections is to withdraw attention from the only possible source of genuine, though limited, control—that by human beings themselves. The realization that since Boundless Existence has no properties of its own that work either for good or ill with respect to human life obliges us to focus on ourselves, both individually and collectively, as agents for both understanding and exercising limited areas of control over the character of our own interactive meanings. In opposition to these prevalent, religiously inspired views concerning where to look for sources of enlightenment or salvation, the thesis argued for here, as based on a realization of the characterlessness of Boundless Existence, stresses instead a commitment to reinforcing and giving heightened attention to the character—the natural conditions of and limited human resources for effective control of—interactive meanings realized between the limits of birth and death for human existents. This genuine, though limited, control is to be sought, and is in fact increasingly found, by the exercise of sound intellectual methods (e.g., those of science) in understanding the interactions of existents, and by effectively applying such understanding under the guidance of experimentally tested fruits of the exercise of practical intelligence and scientifically grounded technology.[30]

The Rest Is Silence

At the very beginning of this book, I quoted the remark Wittgenstein makes in his *Tractatus* that "the solution of the problem of life is seen in the vanishing of the problem." If we were to agree with the soundness and depth of this insight on the basis of our own approach to the analysis of "the question about the meaning of life," we might do so on two grounds. In the first place, as the earlier treatment of the notion of interactive meanings has stressed, it is important to surrender the attempt to answer the question about

---

30. For a thorough analysis of this conception of practical intelligence, see the many philosophical writings of John Dewey.

"*the* meaning of life" (what Wittgenstein calls "the problem of life") if one presupposes, in phrasing the question in this way, namely that there is (or is not) *a* meaning to life, that one must try to specify and identify in what it consists. The notion of *the* meaning to life— that it is in some way singular, ultimate, or all-encompassing—is a mirage and wholly gratuitous. To search for it, or with pessimists to bemoan its absence or one's failure to achieve it, is a failure to raise a genuine question. Instead, as my earlier discussion has argued, one should, at best, phrase the question and examine possible answers by using the term "meaning" in its plural form: there are *meanings* of one sort or another in every life of every human existent. The important question is to analyze in what these consist, and what the conditions, methods, and criteria are for the selection, evaluation, maximization or minimization (as the case may be), and degrees of control of the multiplicity of meanings realized or realizable in particular lives. One way of interpreting Wittgenstein's remark, then, about the "vanishing of the problem of life" (and I am not saying this is the way *he* would have chosen, although it is one I would recommend), is the reason I have have just given: one should make the problem vanish by *dissolving* the question or problem, since it ·rests on the unacceptable and misleading presupposition that there is *a* or *the* meaning to be found in life.

However, there is more to be said. For in terms of our earlier analysis, especially when adopting the broadened use of the term "meaning" to allow not only for its application to multiple interactive meanings in the lives of human existents living in the observable universe, but also to include the kind of meaning that is available by becoming intensively aware of Boundless Existence, one could also respond to the question (or problem) of the meaning of life by making it vanish altogether. The awareness of Boundless Existence, as a dimension of Reality ("the world") in which we live, has its own distinctive consequence in making the problem of life vanish. However, what this awareness contributes is not the kind that results from stressing the plural character of interactive meanings. In the present case, the problem vanishes insofar as one has an awareness of the situation of the lives of individual human existents "in" Boundless Existence, and that since Boundless Existence is Nothing, Emptiness, then *in this respect* life has no meaning either.

We have now to investigate what supports this result, and thereby provides another reason for interpreting Wittgenstein's remark about solving the problem of life by making it vanish. To see why an intensified awareness of Boundless Existence, in its own distinctive way, makes the question of the meaning of life vanish, I shall focus on the way in which that awareness is experienced by the cultivation of a special type of *silence*.

Since I shall be engaging in the use of language to explore the character of this special type of silence, it is necessary, of course, to dispel at the very outset what at first glance might be an obvious objection to entering upon such a discussion. "How," it may be asked, "can one clarify or explore the nature of the special character of the type of silence one is interested in by breaking silence and indulging in a flow of words?" The obvious reply to this challenge is to point out that in talking *about* silence, one is not exhibiting silence, undergoing it, or experiencing it. The talk can only give certain pointers or clues to what is involved in having the experience of silence. It does not pretend to, nor can it succeed in, replacing the experience of silence, any more than talk about the taste of a pineapple is a substitute for tasting it, or any amount of musical analysis is a substitute for actually listening to the music. While not a substitute for the experience, language might prove helpful by offering apt analogies or contrasts with other occasions for, and types of, silence. These cautionary remarks about the limitations as well as the possible benefits of talking *about* the silence that accompanies the awareness of Boundless Existence are worth bearing in mind as we proceed to examine the nature of this distinctive experience.

It will be recalled from our earlier discussion of Boundless Existence, according to the world picture which here serves as our guide, that because of its total lack of any properties other than its designating *that* the observable universe Exists (its only "what" is its equivalence to a particular "that"), it is impossible to use ordinary affirmative, literal, propositions that make predicative use of concepts for purposes of description or explanation. For this reason, no claims to knowledge about Boundless Existence are even possible, hence they cannot be evaluated as either true or false. The only access to Boundless Existence is through awareness, not through propositionally formulated applications of concepts to observationally identified materials that, when confirmed, can be said to embody or convey warranted beliefs or knowledge. Since it is not propositional or conceptual, the awareness of Boundless Existence is, to this extent, experienced in silence. If one breaks this silence, it can only be to engage in metaphor, negative statements ("not this, not that . . ."), or exclamations and expressions of feeling evoked by the experience.

With this as our background, we must now consider the consequences of having this experience of enforced silence in responding to the question concerning the meaning of life. In what way, if at all, does it contribute anything new or different from what has already been said in our previous exploration of this topic?

In order to answer this question, we must go beyond the bare statement that the awareness of Boundless Existence (or what amounts to the same thing, the acceptance that it represents as a fundamental, groundless dimension of Reality) does not sustain the use of concepts and propositions to describe it. Specifically, what this blockage of all use of concepts amounts to is the denial that there is any *inherent intelligibility or value* in the Existence of the universe. The Existence of the universe has no structure of any sort that would make possible the exploration and determination (however tentative and incomplete) of this putative structure and a consequent ability to be able to set it out in propositions. Insofar as the very notions of intelligibility and value presuppose the discrimination of component parts and interconnections of one sort or another among such parts, in that which it is claimed possesses intelligibility and value, then Boundless Existence cannot meet these conditions. As distinguished from the universe's being an existent, the Existence of the universe has no discriminable components and no structural interconnection among components. The Existence of the universe is neither intelligible in causal terms nor by exhibiting some designful plan or linkage of means to ends nor by meeting the requirements and conditions of some accepted esthetic, moral, or any other set of criteria and standards. In being empty of *all* properties, Boundless Existence is also void of any causal, teleological, or value-satisfying properties.

This situation of emptiness with respect to intelligibility and value as it holds for Boundless Existence is, of course, wholly different from what is the case with the manifold pursuits, realizations, and satisfactions or frustrations in the search for, and experience of, intelligibility or value in the domain of interactive meanings realized in the course of the lives of human existents. In that domain, understanding of causal connections (whether on the level of common sense or of science), as well as the making of fresh plans or the discernment of the filling out of designs already in existence, are commonplace. There we find endless examples of the achievement of satisfactions (or the failure to reach satisfactions) by human existents in their interactions with one another and with other existents. Hunger and satiety, boredom and excitement, routinized performance and genuine creativity, restricted and shared experience, evil and good, welcome accidents and disastrous ones—these and many other parameters for mapping the course of interactive meanings are everywhere germane, applicable, and reapplicable to the lives of individuals. But they play no role whatsoever insofar as we think of our lives under the aspect of Boundless Existence. Boundless Existence has no powers of its own, no cares or concerns, no standards, no goals, no plans, no order of operation—not even a blind, purely causal one.

If we look at our individual lives, at our accomplishments or failures, at the pleasures and sufferings of others, at the evils inflicted by humans on other humans, at the glorious creative contributions made by exemplary human beings—for example in art and science— all of these, when seen against the backdrop of the meaninglessness of the Existence of the universe and all it contains, take on a quality of meaninglessness. They are not intelligible or valuable in cosmic perspective since the Existence of the cosmos does not own them, explain them, justify them, include them in some overall plan, order, or design.

When we take this perspective, what is there to say? We cannot point to any wider scheme in terms of which the enormous variety of human experiences takes on a role, fills a place, or contributes to our understanding of how or why they are what they are. We must remain silent; there is nothing to say that would give our lives meaning in this cosmic sense because, in living in a world that has the dimension of Boundless Existence, our lives, too, are surrounded by and immersed in meaninglessness. The only sources of genuine, redeeming positive meaningfulness of our lives are on the level of interactive meanings—as human existents living in a universe that is itself an existent, and by interacting with other existents, but whose Existence, in general or in part, is without meaning, without intelligibility or value.

Summing Up

In adopting the view that the principal dimensions of Reality are the existent observable universe and Boundless Existence, a guiding presupposition in my treatment of the question of the meaning of life has been the conviction that a considered response calls for an analysis of the phrase "meaning of life" under the aspect of each of these major ontological dimensions. On the basis of this approach, the qualified and noncontradictory answer I have offered to the question "Does life have a meaning?" has been: yes and no.

Boundless Existence consists in the fact *that* the universe Exists. It marks the ontological locus of the impenetrability by any humanly devised scheme of conceptual bounds to go beyond the awareness of this basic fact. It blocks all attempts to explain *how* or *why* the universe Exists. The failure to achieve intelligibility not only underlies the rejection of any effort to assign a teleological order to the Existence of the universe, it also denies the presence of any scientifically determinable causal intelligibility in such Existence. Awareness of Boundless Existence as a fundamental feature of Reality is tantamount to denying the possibility of making the Existence of the universe intelligible by appealing to any conceptual scheme—whether philosophic, religious, or scientific. Any such scheme, whether purportedly descriptive, explanatory, or valuational, is, from the vantage point of the world picture here advocated, altogether lacking in convincingness or plausibility.

The life of every human existent is filled to a lesser or greater degree with misery, pain, and frustration, thereby reducing or blocking the full realization of positive values on the level of interactive meanings. Whatever progress may be made through human ingenuity and practical control in reducing or alleviating, if not totally eliminating, the sources and conditions of such aspects of life, there is another dimension of it that is altogether beyond human intervention or even limited control—the fact, namely, that the life of every human existent is lived in a world that manifests Boundless Existence on a cosmic scale. Viewed under the aspect of Boundless Existence, the lives of human existents are both unintelligible and lacking in any support or place in any overall designful scheme or intelligible order.

As an existent part of the observable universe, humankind's existence is both intelligible and open to the achievement of positively charged interactive meanings. The answer to the question whether life has meaning is "yes," to the extent that the life of any individual human existent can be made in some degree intelligible, and to the extent that at least some of its interactive meanings are of a welcome, positively charged variety (as judged by relevant humanly adopted and applied criteria) and fall within the range of limited control by human intelligence. As itself an existent, the observable universe offers a foothold (in the sense of providing the conditions and possibilities) to human existents for the realization of human values. The range of interactive meanings and values, while including the achievement of intelligibility, includes much else. With respect to this diversity and multiplicity, the criteria that judge different types of meaning-values are severally different from those that guide or judge purely intellectual goals and achievements. In short, for human beings considered as existents within the observable universe, the meanings of human life can be specified or found, not by claiming to find them in some preassigned cosmic or divine source and authority, but by making human life both intelligible through scientific means and by exercising limited areas of control in maximizing modes of experience chosen on technological, esthetic, affective, and moral grounds for their positively charged meaning-values.

Most importantly, manifold human efforts to *make* life inter-actively meaningful in a variety of directions, through the maximization of positively charged meaning-values, are the only appropriate response to the opportunities and challenges that the gift of life opens up. The efforts and responsibility toward making these efforts succeed belong uniquely and exclusively to human existents themselves.